The Wisdom of

# Buddhist Psychology

## &

## The Heart of

# Buddha's teachings

Explore Four Noble truths & Eightfold Path,
Spiritual Intelligence to improve mental health,
theory of void, & meditation for liberation.

By

Anit Korpal

# Content

# Chapter 01
## Birth of Buddhism

*"Teach this triple truth to all: A generous heart, kind speech, and a life of service and compassion are the things which renew humanity."*

**Buddha**

Around 565 BC, 2500 years ago, a child was born in an Indian north-east kingdom, Lumbini (now located in Nepal). People were not aware, but this child was about to change the world. The whole world's perception of living a safe religious life was about to be shattered with the truth of Liberation.

In Lumbini, King Suddhodana was the leader of a clan called the Shakya. Suddhodana married the princess Maya Gotami and her sister Pajapati Gotami. They were both princesses of another clan called 'Koliya.' Around the mid 5th century BC, Queen Maya had a dream of a white elephant. Which descended from the heavens, gave her a lotus flower, and then magically entered inside her womb. She was surprised and amazed at the details of the dream. But deep within, the queen felt that this dream might mean something. She wanted to know the meaning of such a dream, so she decided to ask the experts at the time, the sages.

When she enquired the sages about it, they explained that a white elephant entering her womb means that she has conceived a pure being from heaven, as her child on that same night.

They made a prediction through the dream that the queen will give birth to a son, who will either become a *Chakravartin* or a 'Buddha' meaning. Chakravartin means 'great ruler' & Buddha means the 'enlightened being.' They explained that their son would either conquer the world as a great king or renounce the world to become enlightened. Any of the two things were possible. They mentioned it was challenging to be sure about what their son might choose to do with his life. As a matter of fact, the child did both; he indeed became enlightened and conquered the world in his own ways.

It is said that the queen did not experience any pain while giving birth to the child of the heavens. She experienced a vision where she stood still while holding the branch of a tree in her right hand, & the gods helped the child come out effortlessly. They named the child 'Siddhartha.' The word 'Siddhartha' is made up of two Sanskrit words, 'Siddha' means 'the one who attains perfection' and 'artha' means an 'objective'. The combination makes 'Siddhartha,' which means 'the one who has attained the highest objective.' Seven days after giving birth to Siddhartha, the queen died. The sister, Pajapati Gotami, raised Siddhartha as her own child, fulfilling all responsibilities of a mother.

As soon as the child was born, the king was afraid that the prophecy of him renouncing the kingdom would come true, so he asked the sages for a solution. He wanted a path that would lead his son straight to become the world's greatest ruler, and this path should lead him away from the sage life. The father wanted to kill all possibilities of him renouncing the world. All the sages worked for days and nights to find out a perfect solution. In the end, they suggested that the young prince must never witness any sign of suffering in this world. Suffering in any form, old age, sickness, or death because these scenes might trigger an existential crisis in him. He could begin his spiritual quest by following this simple curiosity. If he could avoid witnessing such sufferings, only then could he be led to the path of being the greatest ruler in the world. The king accepted the solution and managed to get all the pleasures, education, comfort, and a luxuriously comfortable life around his son in the castle. The king made all possible efforts to show Siddhartha the extraordinary life of wealth, luxury, and pleasure inside his luxurious castle's impenetrable walls.

King Shudhodhana issued a strict notice to everyone living in the castle. The message mentioned that nobody was allowed to talk about any kind of human suffering to the young prince because these things could trigger the curiosity in Siddhartha. By such strict efforts of his father, he has entirely driven away from the real world of suffering, miseries, pain, sickness, and even a single thought of death. He had no idea about the whole lives lived outside that castle. In fact, he never had a view of suffering or dying in his entire life lived in this castle.

At the age of 16, he was married to 'Yashodhara' who was also 16 years old. She was daughter of King Suppabuddha, and Amita. It is being said that Yashodhara was among the most beautiful girls in the whole kingdom. After a few years of their marriage, they had a son. They named him 'Rahula.' His father built a perfect life, and he was living a life full of all kinds of pleasures around him throughout the day and the night. But fate was decided, and his life was about to change. When all his pleasures started fading, the prince's heart started longing to see the world outside the castle. Somehow, he found out about some exciting event in the village away from the castle, and he decides to go there at night. It was just his reason to leave the castle for one night, without intimating his father.

In the middle of the night, the young prince left the castle on his cart. He was accompanied by his charioteer named 'Channa.' Channa was amongst the servants who received that notice to avoid any topic of pain, suffering, or death in front of the prince. He was also not allowed to share any truth about human sufferings with the prince. On the way, The young prince Siddhartha saw an old man. He wondered why the man looked different from the castle's young people. He asked his charioteer about him; Channa tried to distract and deny to answer, as he was afraid to break his father's rule. But Siddhartha assured him not to fear the father because he wanted to know the truth. Finally, Channa told Siddhartha that everyone gets old; age is the eternal truth. Every year, we move a little closer to being old. Your father, You, me, and everyone we know will get old & weak just like this man."
Channa explained, and then he realized that the body is designed to decay. He discovered this body will get old and that all its beauty, powers, and charm is lost. He could see that the body has to bear weakness & physical decay. Life would not always be lively and young, as it was for him at the time. He could see that life would still be so full of pleasures.

They kept going towards their destination; after walking for a while, the prince saw a sick, coughing, weak man, and he wondered what happened to him. He asked Channa, and the charioteer told the prince, "this man is sick; his body suffers from a disease." He made it clear that anyone with a human body is prone to such diseases. Channa further explained that not only the body gets weaker with time, but also it might experience sickness. He realized that our bodies are designed to be sick. He could clearly see that we can't control everything in this life, & losing pleasure is nothing but a matter of time. We could get a disease at any point in our life, and we will have to bear the pain that comes with it. He finally understood that this life is not a time of pleasure to be spent in this world; the pain is also a part of this life, and suffering is an ever-shining truth.

They kept going. On the way, he saw a dead man carried away in a temporary wooden flat on four individuals' shoulders. He couldn't comprehend what was happening, so he asked Channa again. He explained that everyone, including the young prince, will die one day. Before this day, he never knew that our lives would come to an end. Channa explains that this man has expired, and he is not alive anymore. He further explains that the body is now being taken to the cremation ground, where it will be burnt traditionally. Siddhartha always believed pleasure and luxury to be the truth of life, but now he saw that the ultimate truth is, 'It ends.' Life was meant to end, everyone dies one day, then what is the point? He wondered. What are we doing here? He wondered if life has so much impermanence, then why are we here?

The prince goes into deep thought, wondering about all the sufferings. He asks his charioteer one more question, which turns out to be the most important realization for him. The prince asked, "It will happen to me as well" Channa replied, "This will happen to everyone." Channa explains that everyone who is born as human life gets sick and definitely dies one day. In fact, everyone we know will die, and that is the end of this life. We have this life, and this body, as an impermanent gift that will be taken away one day. The prince is utterly shocked and doesn't know what to do.

Various existential questions covered his mind. The prince had his fourth encounter of a meditating sage. At the prince's request channa explained, this man was seeking something permanent beyond this body; he searched for the eternal truth. He has renounced the usual lifestyle of society, family, and attachments. Channa explained further that the sage has left all the luxuries and all attachments to seek life's permanent truth. He realized that a sage is the one who had renounced the world to seek something permanent & to seek the eternal truth. After these encounters, he could no longer enjoy the luxurious artificial life of pleasure inside the castle. His father spent 29 years keeping him stuck in the illusion of luxury, pleasure, sex, relationships, comfort, and power. His fate still brought him to where he belonged. Siddhartha immediately knew that he wished to pursue the truth, and the only way was to renounce his normal life.

Even though his father did his best to avoid the interaction of sufferings with the prince, he encountered people with their respective sufferings and realized a lot about life. For the first time, he saw the outside world in its natural forms. He experienced life outside of the castle's artificial life. He saw an old man, a sick man, a dead body, and a meditating sage. These interactions were enough for him to realize that this life is impermanent, and he needs to seek the eternal truth.

At the age of 29, he bid a silent farewell to his father, sleeping wife, and son and finally left the castle in the middle of the night. He took his trustworthy horse with him, 'Kanthak,' & rode on him for almost 6 miles. He left the horse & turned away to renounce his old life. He renounced the horse, his castle, his family, and luxuries to begin his spiritual quest for the ultimate truth of life.

He went into the forest, and there he found 5 ascetics who were practicing severe asceticism and torture on themselves. He was looking to begin his spiritual journey, so he decided to join them. For 6 years, he practiced extreme asceticism with them; he ate one rice grain for a meal, starved himself, and practiced all difficult rituals. He bore all the tortures and rituals he was aware of, renouncing food and meditating for days without eating, but it didn't help him. Soon, he realized that he is becoming physically weak; he felt he was about to die without finding the answer to his questions.

Finally, he decided to leave the practice and went away in search of the truth again. He reached another place in the forest, where he found a bodhi tree; he sat below and started meditating. A woman came to him and offered him some porridge; he politely accepted. Only after eating and meditating properly he could continue his quest. Now, he decided that he would not get up until he found the answers to his questions. He decided that he will stay here until he finds what is permanent in this life until he finds what the eternal truth is. Ultimately, He kept meditating and got awakened under the bodhi tree. He got enlightened and became 'The Buddha.' He was also known as the Shakyamuni Buddha; Shakya is the one who belongs to the clan of Shakyas and Muni means the sage, Shakyamuni means 'the sage of the shakyas.'

After enlightenment, he felt free of all attachments and was liberated in the true sense. Now, he knew that he had to free the whole world from the same suffering that everyone passed on from generation to generation. So, he decided to teach his way of meditation to seek the truth to everyone. He began his journey to find his first disciples. He ended up in front of the same 5 ascetics whose company he renounced earlier, the ascetics who believed that extreme austerities were the only way to enlightenment. They mocked the Buddha, and denied taking any lessons from him. But when Buddha spoke, his appearance, and his speech, made them listen. In this meeting, they realized that the man was not the same anymore; they felt that he had found something they have not found yet. In fact, they knew Buddha had found something that they failed to find, and they happily became his first disciples. Buddha taught them that extreme pleasures are not the way to lead a life, but in the same way, extreme pain is also not the way to liberate from the sufferings. Both luxury and torture, are equally poisonous, and only a middle way could lead them to enlightenment. The same teachings were incorporated to become the 4th most followed religion globally, 'Buddhism.'

After thousands of years, Buddhism is taught in various schools with the knowledge maintained in the Sutras. As per the Mahayana school of Buddhism, Buddha is not the name of 'Gautam Buddha,' but in many sects of Buddhism it is treated as a title. Buddha, means the one who awakened, and therefore anyone can become a buddha. In fact, there is a buddha in all of us, we just need to lose all layers of coverings of illusion, to find the true buddha-nature inside us. Once we lose all fake conditioning that covers us all our lives, the only thing that remains in the end is the 'Buddha Nature.'

Buddha is the word of inspiration. Buddhism is a simple religion, with simple positive rules of life that gradually clean the mind. In fact, Buddhism aims to clear the garbage of the mind, clean it completely, and then proceed with a clear view of the world. This cleaning of mind leads to inner peace, and this peace turns the practice of Buddhism easier for the beginning. We all are aware that peace is difficult to create, especially in our modern world. We have different social media platforms, movies, songs, toxic news, people, and so many other things. It becomes extremely difficult to keep the mind in a peaceful zone. Once we let the toxicity outside affect us inside, it gets deeper and deeper. It thus ruins our peace and any future possibility of peace. So, how can we create some permanent peace within our hearts? Some peace that will help us relax, amidst the difficulties of life, will help us live this life completely. As per Buddhism, there is a way towards eternal peace within this life. The middle way, the meditation way, the four noble truth way, and the eightfold pathway. No matter what we call it, it all leads to the same point of meditation.

Meditation is to breed peace. In Mahayana Buddhism, anyone can become a Buddha. It is only a matter of realizing the true buddha-nature of oneself. In Hinayana Buddhism, One can only reach enlightenment for oneself, but cannot become a Buddha. The practitioner can only reach the highest level to become an Arhats. In different sects of Buddhism, they define Buddha differently. Some treat Buddha as an idol figure, to treat him as an inspiration for this spiritual journey. Some treat him as a Liberation state, a title to be achieved at the end of this journey. None of it is wrong, but it brings out a different mindset in the journey, therefore one must choose the school to follow wisely. Apart from the definition, there are different types of Buddhas.

- **The Buddha:** Buddhas are the ones who are perfectly enlightened. The ones who have found the eternal truth. The one who is free from all limitations of the mind, and thus has received enlightenment. Buddhas are the ones with the purest minds, free from all obstructions of the thoughts, and have the purest hearts. They are free from all corruption of the world. As per Mahayana Buddhism, all beings' true nature is the Buddha nature, i.e., the nature of Liberation or the pure being. Once the being can free themselves from the hindrances formed by the mind, the only thing that remains is the being's true nature. The only thing that remains is the Buddha-nature. The only thing that remains is the state of 'Nirvana,' also called the state of 'enlightenment.' A Buddha has limitless compassion for all beings in the universe, and unmatched wisdom within himself. The Buddha is perfection, there is nothing to be attained after attaining Buddhahood.

- **The Arhats:** The Arhats are the ones who meditate to enlighten themselves only. Mahayana Buddhism defines arhats as those who have excelled far ahead in the spiritual path, but they did not reach full Buddhahood. Different sects see arhats differently, but it simply means someone who is in search of enlightenment. Different schools of Buddhism have different views about the enlightenment of arhats. Different schools define their Buddhahood differently. Someone who is seeking the eternal truth is an Arhat. Buddha himself was an Arhat, before he became Buddha, as he was on his path to enlightenment. In simple language, the Arhats are the ones who renounce the world to seek enlightenment. In Theravada tradition, An arhat is the highest state to reach, and one can not become a Buddha. As per Mahayana, there are stages to be complete even after becoming an Arhat, therefore one must continue the search and keep moving towards attaining the full Buddhahood for reaching complete enlightenment.

- **The Bodhisattvas:** The Bodhisattvas enlighten themselves as well as others. They are the ones who have renounced the attachments of normal lives, and invested sincerity to attaining enlightenment. But they are aware of the sufferings of other beings. So they either teach the world after attaining full Buddhahood, or they delay their complete Buddhahood for the sake of guiding others towards nirvana. Though they are enlightened, they still need to teach others, to help others release from the eternal suffering of life. They teach others about what they have attained, how they have attained it, and work towards freeing them from their sufferings.

- **The pratyekabuddhas:** One more type of Buddha is the Pratyekabuddhas, most people never heard about them, they are the hermits who retreat from the world to enlighten themselves. They are also enlightened beings, but they keep their enlightenment to themselves. They do not make it their responsibility to enlighten others. They are not aware of other beings' sufferings, or they are not interested in freeing others. The Pratyekabuddhas reach enlightenment through their own efforts, and are also known as the silent teachers. If they decide to teach others, they teach their disciples through their own experiences only. According to Mahayana Buddhism, Pratyekabuddhas and Arhats are the ones who didn't reach complete Buddhahood. Though, this opinion also differs in different sects of Buddhism.

Anyone who is looking to move towards buddhism could begin his journey with the three jewels of Buddhism. The three jewels of Buddhism discussed the three support systems for someone who decides to take the path of Buddhism. These support systems are the refuge for Buddhism. 'Refuge' is a word that is used in different contexts here. From the moment we are born, we take refuge in all our actions to avoid responsibilities. We take refuge from our mother, our friends, our father, from all our relationships & even our home. As we grow old, we take refuge in our habits, our addictions, money, religion, power, and even the conditioning of our mind. This refuge is the support that we need to avoid any reality, and continue our lives in illusion. We lean on this support, to exploit it.

These refuges bind the man in his own self, by creating limitations that couldn't be broken by our mind. A Buddhist must take a different refuge, which is not a support to lean over. Still, it is a support to have a fulfilling journey of enlightenment. A Buddhist must renounce the usual circus of life. To avoid being reborn in such suffering, they must be ready to take refuge in these three jewels of Buddhism, The Buddha, The Dharma, & The Sangha.

You must have heard such a mantra from a Buddhist monk,

*Buddham Saranam Gacchami, Dharmam saranam gacchami, Sangham saranam gacchami*

In Sanskrit, 'saranam' means 'refuge', & Gacchami means 'I go'.

So, the text means,

I go for refuge to the Buddha (awakened one/teacher),

I go for refuge to the Dharma (teachings),

I go for refuge to the Sangha (community).

Let us dive into little more details about each one of them:

- **I go to the Buddha for refuge.**

  Buddha here represents Gautam Buddha, but all the Buddhas and Bodhisattvas who are the torchbearers for the disciples. When a disciple takes refuge within Buddhism, buddhas are the first to become the pillars of support, inspiration, & blessings. The Buddhas guide us as teachers and inspire us to embark on this Liberation journey to detach from this human life's continuous sufferings.

- **I go to the Dharma for refuge.**

  Dharma represents the complete teachings of Buddha. It includes all sutras, scriptures, texts, and even the oral teachings shared amongst all Buddhist schools. It is the teachings & the path of Liberation shown by the Buddhas and the Bodhisattvas. The scriptures provide us with an abundance of wisdom and opportunity to learn from them. The stories, and analogies explain everything about Buddhism, the eightfold path, and nirvana. The teachings of the four noble truths, three universal truths, five precepts, and the eightfold paths, are all-inclusive in Buddhism's teachings.

- **I go to the Sangha for refuge.**
Sangha means the community of monks, nuns, and Buddhists following the Dharma. Sangha is there to support the travelers of this path. The ones who are seeking Liberation will have to go through tremendous efforts, and investment of time. They will need extraordinary support in each step of their journey. Unfortunately, a teacher cannot always be that consistent support. Sangha can be that consistent support required to keep the motivation alive in the disciples for the sake of keeping the search alive. The purpose of Sangha is to uplift each other. And the whole community together towards the upliftment of the being.

Buddhism explains that Liberation is a very personal journey. Still, the Sangha's support, teachings of the Dharma, and blessing of the Buddha, can only make it easier for the disciple. As one excels in this path, they get closer to Liberation & their efforts count in the Sangha's upliftment. One who takes refuge in these three jewels is meant to be undertaken as a part of the Buddhist community and can seek the truth and others on a similar journey. After an appropriate amount of time, the same person can inspire others to take refuge among these three jewels and start their own journey for seeking the ultimate truth.

*"Know well what leads you forward and what holds you back, and choose the path that leads to wisdom."*

**Buddha**

# Chapter 02

# The Buddhist life

*"Believe nothing, no matter where you read it, or who said it, no matter if I have said it, unless it agrees with your own reason and your own common sense."*

**Buddha**

*Part 01:* **The Five Precepts**

The panchshila, Pancasila is a Sanskrit word, where 'Panch-' means five, and '-Shila' means principles or in this context precepts. The five precepts are the preliminary conditions to begin one's journey of Liberation through Buddhism. They can be considered little baby steps towards a Buddhist journey. Which helps prepare one's mind, mindset, thought process, and even the body for Liberation's pure journey.

These five conditions are to be fulfilled every day, it must be embraced as a mindset to live a Buddhist life. They are the code of ethics, that makes humans better and safe for beings and nature. These five points are a way to cultivate peace for ourselves, and everything around us. Let us dive deeper into these points:

1. **No Killing:** The first precept is a life-affirming condition. It implies respect for life in all its forms. A living being is nothing but life witnessing life. If we can not respect the life inside us, which is the reason for us being alive here, how can we live life completely? The respect for life must begin with the life inside us, we may clearly see that we are only a life tool. After we respect life in ourselves, we must extend this respect to other humans' lives. Because there is literally no difference between the life inside us and other human beings' lives. After paying respect to all humans, we may extend our respect to other beings of the universe. Animals, mammals, insects are all sentient beings of the universe. Life in humans is no different than the life in them. After paying respect to all the living beings, one may even try to advance this respect to nature's non-living things. Like the plants, the planets,

the stars, the sun, and the moon, we wouldn't have any human lives without any of these things. This respect goes deeper and deeper, and it will only strengthen our sense of being. This respect is the seed of immense gratitude in ourselves, as it helps us see that we are one with nature. There is no separation, and thus there should not be any discrimination as well.

No killing is the most important precept. Any form of killing is proportional to an insult to life and the living. Any form of harm to other beings comes back as Karma, and draws one away from Liberation. Suppose we practice Buddhist philosophy, and still kill other beings. In that case, it simply means that we do not understand the essence of Buddhism. It also means that we have not cultivated the essential respect for this life. Without such respect, there can not be a deep sense of gratitude towards life. Without this gratitude, all our meditation practice feels empty and delayed. No killing implies, no killing of other humans, or any other sentient beings as well. The pain & suffering we cause to others, come back to us in some form. The whole concept of Buddhism lies around the understanding of suffering and reduction in the causes of suffering. Buddhism believes in Karma, and so harming any sentient being is an open invitation for the same suffering for ourselves. This can be understood by the fact that a buddha sees everyone as himself. Everyone is equal, and one. Therefore, it seems ridiculous to intentionally harm other beings, because it will just mean that we are unintentionally harming ourselves. Buddhism teaches us to respect life, sentient beings, ourselves, and nature. The more we respect, the more gratitude is breeding in us, and this gratitude is the first learning of Buddhism. This is a golden first step, in the long journey of awakening.

2. **No stealing:** Stealing means taking something that does not belong to us. It is clear that taking something that someone else has earned with hard work, is ethically wrong. Stealing from others, taking away someone else is property is an act of greed. There can not be a pure practice of meditation, if we allow ourselves to act through greed present in our

hearts. We must see this greed clearly, and minimize it little by little every day. This greed is harmful to society, and for the individual being as well. The one who flows with the need of greed, can not turn to Buddhism for Liberation. The act of stealing does not suffice one is greed, but it enhances the greed exponentially. The more you steal, the more you want. The cycle goes on and on. There is no satisfaction. We have seen some debaters talking about stealing for feeding, some poor people steal because they do not have enough. The argument is not appropriate because, if all poor people started stealing the world would live in chaos. In fact, this alone will lead to a greater distance between the rich and the poor. This alone would never allow any poor to earn enough. This structure will collapse on the heads of all poor people, therefore they must not listen to their greed, and only work as much as possible. If they stay true to their efforts and works, their heart will be at peace. They won't need any stealing with this attained peace because stealing might bring something today, but it takes something tomorrow. It brings rewards today, but it takes away the inner peace. We may not forget that stealing is just a matter of scarring the karmic board with some bad remarks. We must keep our Karma clear from all bad energies. As per Buddhism, this can cause our Liberation to drift far away from us. In this life, and even in the future lives. Therefore, stealing in any form, taking what doesn't belong to us, is an act of stealing. Such acts include frauds, scams, forgery, deceiving customers, taking money without asking, not returning your loan etc.

This precept is aimed to teach one to respect others' property. Only when we learn to respect, we may minimize the sense of comparison within ourselves. This sense of comparison is the biggest cause of our useless needs, and greed. This comparison makes us think of stealing in the first place, such thought is what turns a normal man into a thief. These thoughts generate out of disrespect, and comparison, it is the true power behind every thief. When we see it clearly, it becomes impossible to compare ourselves with someone else.

3. **No misconduct:** This percept teaches us to observe all our desires without any judgment. Only after we watch and observe closely, we can make an effort to end those desires. This step is just a preparation for the silence of the mind, whenever it comes up with a foolish plan to fulfill a desire. No misconduct means any desire that has the potential to lead us towards harming ourselves, others, our character, or our lives. If we think about it, all desires have such harmful potential. So, this understanding helps us prepare for the silence of the mind, in our coming journey of Buddhism. Because, when the mind asks you to fulfill a desire, it promises you some pleasure in return. But once we observe the desire, and this promise, we realize that this promised pleasure is also a cause of our suffering. Then, we have no choice but to stop giving in to this promise of this fake pleasure. Now, this way, we learn to respect the purity of our minds. We learn to respect our pure nature. We would not prefer to allow ourselves to be drawn into any act of passion, desire, excitement, and pleasure. This precept is more focused on avoiding adultery, & sexual misconduct. It must be made clear that Buddhism does not talk about avoiding sexual experience. Still, it only suggests that we should not act in excitement to receive some sexual benefits out of the situation. One must not compromise character, discipline, or decisiveness for the sake of sex. Many teachers have mentioned that consensual sex between adults is considered very normal in Buddhism. It is not considered a sin at all. Some sects of Buddhism consider this precept to be closely related to sexual misconduct only. Still, it is truly discussing all passions & desires that have the potential to make us flow in the wrong direction. In our modern times, sexual misconduct has risen in numbers, so the teachers prefer to consider putting more focus on those desires. But in reality, this point includes all desires that cause one to lose their character, and act in excitement.

4. **No lying:** Buddhism is not a religion in its true sense because it is not just a way to find Liberation. But it is also an ideal way of living a human life. Following the path of Buddhism can bring peace to all humans & the whole of humanity as well. This precept teaches us to use our speech with honesty. Any part of speech that includes lying, deceit,

misdirection, misleading and scamming with our words, must be avoided at all costs. It creates bad Karma in our Karmic records, and also creates consequences within this life. Practically, we have experienced the bad results of the lies that we spoke in our past. Lies have the potential to ruin a life, a relationship, a business, and it can easily ruin us internally. Lying makes others lose faith in us. If lying becomes an addiction, the person also loses faith in himself. No matter what he does, he will always doubt everyone around him. If you have little belief in yourself, it becomes impossible to trust others. An individual living a life of lies, sucked in his own misbeliefs, living in mistrust, can never even think of attaining something pure. Lies are comfortable initially, and the ones who are addicted to comfort fall into such traps easily. They never wonder that this trap gets them stuck by demanding more and more lies to cover up the earlier lies. Thus begin the cycle of lies, which traps the being deeper & deeper, making it impossible for one to get out of it. Sometimes, an individual gets sick of his own lies, and decides to get out of this trap, and Buddhism provides help for such people. Through the gradual understanding of one's own lies, it gets easier to avoid lying. This behaviour leads us to more content, trustful and healthy living. If someone wishes to reach their true Buddha nature, then the lies have no place inside him. People lie to protect themselves, their desires, and their emotions. All these things are a part of the coverings that we need to lose. For the sake of reaching the Buddhahood. It is not just about enlightenment, we all may realize through experience that lies are followed by suffering. Suffering attracts a reaction, then reaction attracts more suffering. Therefore, it is much better to avoid lying at all costs, to avoid the suffering that lying breeds within our lives. Basically, this precept teaches us that humans must lead a life with honesty. It should respect honesty in all beings, in all its forms.

5. **No intoxicants**: Intoxicants are an excuse to escape from the reality of the world. The one who escapes the real world cannot reach the real buddha nature. In our times, intoxicants have become a sign of class, fun, and good life. Though, we deeply know that all intoxicants ruin our inner system. They intoxicate the purity inside us. They spoil any hope of

decisiveness and sincerity required to walk any pure path in life. People who have seen such dangerous elements' toxicity would never dare to allow them to enter their bodies. Human beings are physically sentient beings, and every action begins with the body. If we wish to purify our existence, it also has to begin with the body. As we understand, purifying the body is easier to begin and track. Though, the difficult part is to purify the mind, once the body works, the mind follows. Therefore, to begin the thought of following Buddhism or any other purity path, one must consider first to purify the body. Avoiding intoxicants is the first step, towards this purification.

To unleash your true self, clarity of mind is absolutely essential. When we respect the clarity of mind, only then can the mind stop chattering. All the above precepts are doing nothing but stopping the mind is chattering. Alcohol, Drugs, Coffee, Weed, or LSD, any drugs that you have ever heard of, what they do? They will make the mind so relaxed that it can't focus on the chattering. But it helps only for a while. Now you know, when you drink too much alcohol or even coffee, the next the mind feels lethargic. Why? It happens because our mind gets out of the mind, by a force of intoxicants, this force hurts afterward. If we want to get out of the mind, peacefully and forever. We need to quit using force on it, because the mind knows how to take revenge on the force you used on itself. Allow it to calm down, through the use of five precepts, and get ready for a journey of Liberation. All the conditions mentioned are the causes of chattering and suffering. As soon as we embrace these precepts, our mind starts to calm down, as it has no content to play with. If you notice closely, most of the time our mind is chattering with the content that we have collected through the wrongdoings of some sort. These wrongdoings breed fear, and the mind keeps itself occupied with that fear.

*"Words have the power to both destroy and heal. When words are both true and kind, they can change our world."*
**Buddha**

Bhava-chakra, is the Buddhist wheel of life & death. It has various different parts that represent the essence of Buddhist teaching. We will study and understand each part in detail. We will begin with the center and move outwards towards all other parts of the circle.

In the center of the bhavacakra, there are three animals, a cock, a snake and a pig, chasing each other from tail to tail. The animals represent the three poisons of human life, ignorance, the attachment to pleasure and aversion. This center is what moves the whole cycle. This is the center of poison, this is the cause of motion in the whole wheel. These poisons are the ones to act as fuel for this eternal cycle of life & death.

Just over the center circle, there is the first concentric circle with half white-half dark background inside it. The white part shows the beings on the right path of enlightenment, who are full of kindness, love, gratitude, humility & compassion. These beings are the ones who do not get involved with any bad karma. They move towards enlightenment with every rebirth, because of their karmic cleaning. On the darker side of this circle, are the beings full of hatred, desires, lust, attachments, & greed. Through these actions, they have driven away from Liberation. They are doomed to be stuck in this cycle of rebirths, over and over again.

Outside this second circle, there is a second concentric circle which shows six different states of existence, including all rising & falling of beings as per their actions in life. The actions are recorded as the Karma in the name of those beings. These six states shows six different realms of existence, as detailed below:

1.  **THE GOD REALM:** This is the realm of the heavenly beings. These are the beings who were rewarded for the good Karma in their past forms of existence. These beings live in a pure land away from our world, where there is no suffering, no pain, no sorrow, and no evil. They enjoy a consistent joy throughout their lives, it is heaven. It is said that life in heaven lasts for about 30,000 years of human time. Though these beings

are not totally safe, they also get reborn in some realms of existence after living for the allowed time in the heavens. In the bhavacakra, you may see a picture of Buddha holding a musical instrument. This depicts the joy of music, within the beautiful scenery of nature. The picture depicts heaven, where Buddha is enjoying the music of existence within himself.

2. **THE DEMIGOD REALM:** This is the realm of Asuras, also known as the Devils. Where there is a day, there must be a night. Nature has a balance for everything. The demigods are opposed to the gods, and therefore are living in consistent war with them. They are full of greed, lust, attachments and envy, they are the depiction of the evil in the universe. They live with a purpose of taking away from the gods. No one desires a birth in such a realm, although it is inevitable that our wrong deeds may make us end up there. In the bhavacakra, we may see a picture of asuras fighting, angry & breeding chaos, anger, fight, violence and evil. Here we see a Buddha holding a sword. This represents the fighting nature of the beings in the asura realm of existence.

3. **THE HUNGRY GHOST REALM:** This is the 'preta' realm, which translates to the hungry ghosts. This realm is similar to hell's realm, here also the ghosts suffer for their past Karma and the wrong deeds. But they do not suffer the hell realms' torture, the ghosts mostly suffer from hunger and thirst. Ones who were full of greed, and envy in their past existences, end up here. It is also believed, the ghosts are in the same places where they used to live before their death. But without being seen by any known or loved ones. So they might see the world going on without them. Which could also be one of their sufferings. In the bhavacakra, we see the Buddha standing around, ghosts with thin necks, fighting, burning and dead. These depict that sudden death can make one enter this realm because of unfulfilled desires. These beliefs are very similar to the Hindu beliefs of Ghosts, and death. Like the hell realm, this

existence is undesirable. Only good karmic records can guarantee the next life away from this realm of existence.

4.  **THE HELL REALM:** Hell is another realm of existence, where we bear the punishment for all our wrong deeds, sins, and negative karmas. In many religions, especially Hinduism and Buddhism, there is a specific punishment for a specific sin. The punishments are severe, torturous, disgusting, and they last for about 60,000 years of human time. After completing the decided punishment, the sinner is free of the negative Karma. They could enjoy a rebirth within a higher realm of existence. In the bhavacakra, we see the Buddha in the middle of all punishments. Here sinners are getting cooked, stabbed, fried, boiled & sawed. The picture implies that every wrong and right action has its consequences. Since nothing is lost in the universe, all our Karma comes back to us, in some form, and we will have to face it. This realm shows us that we can not run from our negative actions, so we must be careful whatever we do here. This can also depict how the whole of humanity suffers, when people choose to do wrong over right. This can also be explained, people choosing hatred over compassion, greed over humility, lust over peace, and money over contentment. Therefore, we must do our best to avoid such actions. They can lead us to any of those realms that make us attend the insufferable punishments, and thousands of years of torture & pain. We must try to walk the path of right deeds. We must intentionally choose the path of truth and Liberation in the life we live so that this journey can advance from here to higher realms.

5.  **THE ANIMAL REALM:** The animal realms are away from enlightenment as they don't have the consciousness and understanding required to embrace this life's intelligence. Beings of this realm only live to survive, food is the goal of their days and survival is their purpose. Their lives are built on the day to day struggles, which revolve around basic acts of living. They do not have the heightened sense to

understand enlightenment or pursue it. Though there are some cases when an enlightened being claimed that animals did reach Liberation amongst their company, it happens only in very rare cases. It is generally believed to be impossible to liberate from the cycle of life and death, if you are born in the animal realm. Although, we might see for ourselves that the animal realm has the beings that suffer the most. But when you think about it, their physical sufferings and struggles are at par with the emotional sufferings. They follow their instant instincts, and generally they are not the decision-makers of their actions. They just do whatever is beneficial in the present moment. In the bhavacakra, we see Buddha's picture, surrounded by wild animals on one side and the domestic animals on the other. It showcases us the two sides of animal realms, domestic and wild. The animal realm is full of suffering, so the picture also shares a message of humanity, co-existence, and compassion towards animals.

6. **THE HUMAN REALM:** This is the only realm, where we get to live freely, enjoy emotions and comfort. We are free to be our own decisions makers as per our intelligence. We are responsible for making life choices that will decide the next realm of our existence. The joy we receive in this life is mostly because of the past good deeds we have done. When a being completes their time in the animal realm, hell realm, or the realm of the demigods, they end up in the human realm. They get a chance to fulfill their Karma and reach the higher realms of existence. In some Buddhist sects, human life is just an opportunity to make decisions out of pure being, and move towards the end of this life-death cycle. As we discussed, the only way to move towards the end of this cycle, is by moving towards Liberation. Suppose we have started a Liberation journey in our past human life, or our past existence in any other realm. In that case, that means we can use this life to be finally liberated from the cycle of life and death. In the bhavacakra, we see a buddha standing in the middle of the picture with human living scenes around. The picture depicts old age, sickness,

working, living with animals etc. This picture implies that every human should experience the essential aspects of a human life, and ultimately practice the essential decisions to attain Buddhahood. We are the only beings full of emotions, compassion, and the power to liberate from the illusion. The heaven realm and the human realm are the only desirable realms for the world's beings, others are full of torture, & pain.

Let us move a little more outwards in the circle, we have the third concentric circle showing the 12 states in the causality chain. This circle depicts 12 scenes that explain the 'cause and effect' nature of this life. Buddhism clearly explains that life is suffering, and every suffering has a cause. The first one is birth. The birth picture depicts that birth is the first cause of all the sufferings & the highest suffering of all, the death. All 12 scenes lead to the next one, it is an unending chain that breeds suffering with each step. There is no escape from this cause and effect. Because every effect leads to another cause, and every cause leads to another effect. The only escape is Liberation, which resides outside of the Bhavacakra.

When the Buddha got enlightened, he saw this picture clearly. He understood that the life-death-rebirth is not a linear progression of time, but it is a cycle. This cycle would not stop until there are sincere efforts to stop all causes, and effectively stop all the coming effects. Outside this third circle, there is a demon' Maara, who is the epitome of time & death, he is the one holding the whole Chakra. It depicts that this demon is playing with the Chakra to create this illusion of time and death. This illusion is the one that drives people away from their true Buddha nature. On the top right corner of this picture, you may see Buddha's picture, pointing to the moon. It means Buddha is away from this Chakra of life-death, and he is enlightened already. The moon is the depiction of Liberation, freedom from life.

Bhavachakra is one of the most relevant pictures in Buddhism, so it is instructed to be placed in every Buddhist monastery. This picture helps people see, observe and understand the current illusions of their life. It is the best way to inspire them to come out of the illusions. It is the central inspiration of all Buddhist teachings.

We must discuss a few other essential parts of the bhavacakra in the following section.

a. **The Centre (The fuel of the Chakra):** Which showcases three animals chasing each other's tails. The pig is chasing the snake tail, the snake chasing the cocks tail, and the cock chasing the pig is tail. These three animals depict aversion, attachment & ignorance. These animals are mere representations of evil thoughts, evil motivations, evil goals, evil deeds, and evil self inside all of us. It implies that all of our sufferings begin with the feelings of hatred we manufacture within ourselves. The center is the force that rotates the whole Chakra and begins the play of life. The center is the main fuel to the whole karmic board, which leads to the trap of life-death. The closer we move towards the center of evil, the farther away from getting out of the circle.

b. **The Buddha (The enlightened one):** The Buddha is standing at the picture's top right corner. He is not linked to the bhavachakra, in fact he is standing outside the bhavacakra. He is enlightened as he got out of this circle by liberating from all the poisons that fuel this circle. He diminished all evil to the level of zero. He arose above from all what could lead to the cause and effect chain. He is now standing with his finger pointing to the moon. The moon represents the state of enlightenment. The picture suggests that we must understand the illusions, and drive of this Chakra. So we can finally move out of this circle, and get closer to the enlightening state of being. The Buddha's finger pointing to the moon depicts Buddha's vision and his guidance towards enlightenment.

c. **The Yama (Lord of the underworlds)**: Some Buddhist teachers mention the devil as the Yama. The Yamaraj who is the one keeping the Karmic records, and the decision-maker of the realms. In Hinduism, he handles the soul after death, and brings justice to the being as per their karmic records. He is the one who holds the whole Chakra, and spins it to create the illusion of life and death. Some Buddhist teachers believe that the Devil is Mara, the demon. He is the one who creates the illusion of time and death, by rotating the Chakra. He keeps all the beings stuck in this game of existence. The name could be different among different sects of Buddhism, but the meaning remains the same.

"All conditioned things are impermanent—when one sees this with wisdom, one turns away from suffering."
Buddha

# Chapter 03
## Buddhist psychology of Life

*"The one who sees me, sees my teaching and the one who sees my teaching, sees me"*
**Buddha**

When Buddha was alive, he realized that there is suffering in every life. In fact, in many of the scriptures, his own words, 'Life is Suffering'. To clarify to laymen like us, he concluded the same thing with every teaching he ever shared. He wished everyone to understand that if everyone could experience the eternal bliss of the true buddha nature, everyone would see all this life as suffering. If we live all our lives in one small room, we would never be able to compare what it feels like to live in a luxurious bungalow.

Similarly, we can have all the fun we can imagine in this human life. Still, we would never compare it to the eternal truth until we get to experience the eternal truth. There is no comparison of this life, with that Liberation. There is no feeling that is close to the feeling of freedom from this circle.

In fact, if one could experience the feeling of eternal bliss, then there would not be anything in the universe that would seem better than the life of enlightenment. But it is not easy to explain, especially to those who have never experienced something different than this life. The ones who are stuck in the trap, can never see the trap. When they exit the trap, they see the whole trap and feel the freedom outside of the trap. In the same way, Buddha came out of the trap, the trap of life-death endless cycle. The trap of time, and once he exited, he could see how blissfully joyful the universe is. He knew that most other humans will just live and die, without ever experiencing anything as blissful as what he experienced. Which is why, as soon as he attained enlightenment. He could visualize that not even in the coming thousand years anyone would reach such Liberation, if he doesn't share his wisdom with others. Buddha shared a lot of his wisdom, and knowledge, because he was a Bodhisattva, and he realized everyone as himself. He wanted to help the world to reach the same state of Liberation just as he did. He felt the suffering of everyone, which made him feel undying compassion for all beings. This intense compassion was why he spent all his life teaching and guiding people towards the noble path of truth.

The suffering that Buddha often mentioned, was not just the sufferings of sorrow, physical pain, or loss of a loved one. Still, they were also the suffering of everything that a human experiences in this life. He talked about pleasure, pain, dreams, wants, ego, fear, achievements, desires, luxuries, and insecurities. Society has advanced in technology, knowledge, relationships, cultures, and science. Still, when we look at the way we live our lives, it hasn't changed much. Society has been stuck in the same cycle of earning and spending money, and fulfilling social responsibilities. Lifestyles have changed. People have different ways of earning and spending money. The structures of families have changed, even the content of their thoughts might have changed a little but deeply, the way of thinking is the same. The cravings for materials, the desires for achievement, the need for sex, and the want for money, are still the same.

The way an individual perceives human life is exactly the same as it was 2500 years ago. We are born, we live, we eat, we survive and we die. Sure, we enjoy the time but is it all that we are here to do? This was what Buddhism denies. According to Buddhism, we are here to seek Liberation. Still, the lives are designed in a way, which pushes us even further away even from self-contemplations. Buddhism is a way to observe the whole circus of life, observe the importance of life, limitations of life, life choices, decisions of life, reality of life, and the eternal truth of life.

Buddhism is different from other religions because it tries to teach us a slightly analytical view to understand the mind. It helps us visualize the process of mind, and observe its functioning. The mind is the creator of this illusion, and it is an illusion itself. When we observe the illusion, from outside of the illusion, it disappears. What exactly is this illusion? This illusion is the feeling of 'I', the ego. The mind creates an ego, and that ego lives life on our behalf. As we discussed, the purpose of all religions in the world, including Buddhism, is to dilute this ego's illusion. There we will begin to live a life free from the ego, free from attachments, and free from all lively distractions. There we explore how to live a life with mindfulness, being present in the current moment because this moment is all there is. When we talk about the mind, Is it such a big problem? What is it?

## What is the mind?

After studying Buddhism we find out, the mind is nothing but a conditioned tool, a series of data, & a process of thoughts. It's a chain of reactions with sufferings attached to its tail. The mind is a mess, it has saved, and analyzed a lot of information inside it, which causes it deadly unrest. The only way to be calm is to bring it to peace by minimizing the functioning, and making it rest. It needs silence to act intelligently, to act full of awareness, & to experience some peace. How can we do it? By using the teachings of Buddhism. Buddhism teachings are easy enough to be understood by anyone. In Buddha's experience, asceticism & religious rituals could not help him answer his questions. He was seeking the ultimate truth. He knew that a man can only begin their journey towards enlightenment only if they are out of their daily lives' worries. If they are sincere towards the journey, they must follow the guidance with all their will. So he laid down his guidance in the simplest form for people like you and me, to follow. Buddha was a visionary, he understood that religion can never elevate a person from its conditioning in all its forms. Most religions in the world were misinterpreted and could only condition people more.

## How did Buddha begin spreading his teachings?

Buddha was aware that he had to share the root information with the disciples, only then could they move upwards to the upliftment. So, Buddha came up with a simple explanation of life, 'Life doesn't end with death'. If life doesn't end with death, it gives life a completely different meaning. In fact, if it doesn't end with death, there must be some more meaning to life than just existing and surviving in our time. The eternal nature of life brings curiosity in the question, it demands the answer to, "Why". Why doesn't life end with death? What is the need for this continuation? To answer these questions, we refer back to the Bhavacakra, the wheel of the life-death cycle. When we clearly understand all these answers, it gives life more hope, that life has something permanent. Though even the body would die in its time, there will be something staying alive, afterwards. To find out what it is? What is it that goes beyond this life? What is it that's permanent? It is nothing but the true being, something that remains after all worldly additions are removed, the buddha nature.

According to Buddhism, a human's life is merely the allowed time meant for using to move towards Liberation. If they fail, they could come back as an animal, or a human, but it would be an eternal cycle just as if caught in a time loop until reaching nirvana. Life has got us caught in the same worries of survival, until we break free getting enlightened. But when practically followed, Buddha's teachings are not only to seek enlightenment. These teachings are ethically ideal that could help a modern man live a peaceful life in our society. Theravada Buddhism explains, three universal truths need to be understood before diving into the Buddhist philosophies. These three are the basis of understanding human life. The Three universal truths are as explained below:

1. Annica (Impermanence)
2. Dukkha (Suffering)
3. Anatta (No self)

1. **Annica:**

*'Whatever arises has to cease. Nothing is lost in the universe.'*
*-Buddha*

Annica is the first universal truth, which translates to impermanence. Buddhist teaching quite often explains this impermanence with the above quote. Buddhist teaching emphasises the thought that nothing in the universe is ever created or destroyed. Just like science states about energy, it is neither created nor destroyed. Body changes with age, feelings change with situations, people change with experiences, our perception changes with time & we change with everything around us. Everything about us is prone to change, life changes, personality changes, & thoughts changes. Even the ideas change, greed changes, lust changes, & everything else that we know, changes. All matter is energy, it converts back to energy, and then again energy creates matter. A tree dies in the soil, and is born out of the soil. In many religions, they feed on soils' products and then they are burnt and mixed with the soil. Cycle of life keeps going. Nothing is permanent in the universe. The whole universe is in a state of flux, consistent variations in all its forms, and constantly changing. Even science makes it clear we are aware that the universe is constantly expanding since it was created. We do not know how fast, or how much, but it expands and changes as the time goes by. Everything changes, life is like a flowing river, ever-changing every moment. Ideas, people, situations, universe, humanity, expressions, feelings, etc., all change. The galaxies collide, black holes collide, the universe keeps destructing itself and creating itself. Which is the proof of impermanence inside us, and outside our world as well.

The whole universe is interlinked, one thing destroys and another is created with the destroyed things' energy. It is like a weighing scale, one end goes down and the other one goes up. Buddhists often explain it like a yin-yang relationship, something amazing happens on one side of the universe, therefore something destructive must be happening on the other side. The universe works in perfect balance, and change is the tool for that balance. This change will always occur at both ends of the thread, as long as life goes on. Therefore, a person experiencing a situation of sorrow today, will experience joy tomorrow, just how life balances itself. Everything is interdependent on other things, we do not exist by ourselves, our birth, life and death everything happens through something else. Change is inevitable.

2. **Dukkha:**

*"The root of suffering is attachment."*
*-Buddha*

The second universal truth is Dukkha, which translates to suffering. Suffering depicts the sorrow, pain, attachment, greed, lust, and everything that ultimately causes suffering. As Buddha explains, suffering is the truth of life, there is no life without suffering. Suffering is part of the process. Since the universe is impermanent and everything changes, the creation consistently experiments with itself, not to find out something, but to experience itself within different forms. Dukkha is the feeling of sadness, boredom, dissatisfaction, restlessness, or a state of disease. There is always some sort of dukkha of the body, or the mind. Hunger, sleepiness, discomfort, Thirst, or Lust, we can not run away from any of it. It arises from the deep unawareness that is born as a result of our spiritual ignorance.

The Buddhist teachers explain Dukkha, as the sufferings that are caused by our sensory experiences. Five aggregates of our body, allows the world to be experienced by us. We turn our experiences into memories and addictions. These addictions are the ones that cause unnecessary attachment to pleasure, even though we are sure that the pleasure and pain will be balanced in all phases of life. This attachment to pleasure is futile, because soon the pain will follow. This pain is the suffering, and the attachment to pleasure is the suffering as well. Buddhism explains suffering, it is not just about the evil parts of life, but also about the good parts that make us crave the pleasure. The little things that turn into desires, and those desires become decision-makers driven by the cravings. The whole functioning becomes such a mess, that decisiveness in our heads turns into a controlled process of steps. Still, we never fix it because we are unable to see the steps or the controller. Sufferings are a part of life, there will be suffering as long as one is stuck in the life-death cycle. There will be no need for Buddhism teachings as long as an individual does not realize the intensity of sufferings, cause of sufferings, and the limitations of the being inside these sufferings. Only after such realisation can one begin a journey towards ending these sufferings. But before starting to observe such sufferings, one must clearly understand the meaning of suffering in the right context. Because Dukkha literally means 'Sorrow', but in the Buddhism context, it does not mean just sorrow. It means all sufferings that cause unrest to our beings deeply. Everything that makes us feel dissatisfied with life makes us feel the deep dissatisfaction with life, and everything that takes away the joy from our lives, is what is meant by the word 'Dukkha'. Only through his context can we conclude that our lives are meant to break the chains of this Dukkha, and get on to a journey of freedom.

3. <u>Anatta :</u>

*"Whatever I can perceive, It is not me, it is not mine, does not belong to me , it is not myself" -Buddha*

Whatever arises must cease. The third universal truth is Anatta, which is often translated as Absence of Self, or No self. You must have heard this famous quote by Rene Descartes, 'I think therefore I am', in the sense of Buddhist studies it is only partially true. In this context, when we stop thinking, the unreal world ceases to exist, but the eternal truth still exists. In fact, when we stop thinking, it begins to shine on us, through us, forever.

Thinking is the process of memory repeating itself, so less thinking means peaceful living. We all have experienced a bad situation where we started talking to ourselves to make the situation worse inside our heads. It does not matter what is happening around us, but our mind is always full of thoughts. We can easily guess that life could be better without talking to myself, thinking to myself and constantly perceiving the universe around me. If we could live without judging the experiences, then we can truly say, "we are free". Buddhists call such a state of mind 'the safe house'. One must observe that thinking is the basis of the personality, which is the cause of all problems. We think, our thoughts create our lives, but our thoughts don't represent us as ourselves. All our thoughts don't belong to the 'I'. This helps us realize that we are not what we remember, & what we experience. This way we can detach ourselves from the experiences. We can detach ourselves from the memories, and it gets easier to look at them. After we look into them completely, we find that we are none of what we have in mind without judgments. We are something beyond all this, we are something that remains after we clear all such elements from our personalities. Only then remain the true being free of all limitations. This state is known as 'Anahata' or Anatta, the state of being, the no-self.

## Conclusion

The thoughts are coming from the kalesha, whatever distracts from meditation is the kalesha. There is darkness and the light inside us, you may remember that story of the wolves. We have two wolves inside our hearts, a good wolf and a bad wolf. They are constantly fighting, which one wins? Well, the one we feed. Simple!
Though, if we study Buddhism's path and follow it with complete sincerity, we might find out that we are neither of these wolves. We are neither darkness, nor the light. We are someone who sees both the darkness and the light. We must understand the three universal truths; through this understanding, an interest will arise. Interest in going beyond the thought by being aware that the thought isn't related to the true

me. This leads to the conclusion that the memory is not me as well. We might find out that the imagination is not me, and everything beyond such things is the real me. All thoughts are begging us to be attached to them, the moment we attach with them we are bound to lose control and flow with these thoughts. But the goal must be to detach from the thoughts and flow freely. Allow the thoughts to arise, and drown by themselves, without holding its tail. Let it come and let it go. Once you stop following the track of thoughts, they lose their importance. They ought to lose their importance and they must lose their importance. Once they lose their importance, they stop showing up unnecessarily, because deep down every thought is full of ego themselves. The mind is a chattering box, all the chatter is distraction for living a present life. Ego gets lazy, ego gets offended, ego pursues thoughts, ego gets greedy, ego gets scared, because ego is attached. It wants to save the perception of being the ego. But the truth is that once it is out exposed, there is nothing it can do. So, it brings out its best effort to protect its lie of existing.

Ego makes us feel like we are standing on the pedestal of ego. It makes us feel like we have to manage our motion as per the limitations of the pedestal, it says we can walk, move, or dance on the pedestal because it is too small, and we might fall. The truth is, we see a pedestal, because we were made to believe there is a pedestal. In reality, there is just us, flowing with nothing to stand on. But that is too much power for us, so we bring down our reality to accept that there must be a base, or how we stay at one place so strongly. Though, the moment we see the ego, it disappears, and there is no pedestal to limit our consciousness's movement. We are free! Finally!

"May all beings have happy minds."

**Buddha**

# Chapter: 04

## Five aggregates & their contribution to the suffering

*"Our life is shaped by our mind; we become what we think. Suffering follows an evil thought as the wheels of a cart follow the oxen that draw it. Our life is shaped by our mind; we become what we think. Joy follows a pure thought like a shadow that never leaves."*

**Buddha**

Suffering has only one cause, which spreads out its branches to different minor causes. The major cause is only one, Attachment, aka Upadana in Buddhism. We have discussed Attachment, the feeling of the need of grasping to grasp something. The grasping doesn't happen on its own, the ego is the tool of grasping. The mind creates the ego, which acts as a machine of attachment, attaching to all emotions, feelings, people, things, and even situations. To end the suffering, one must end the ego, and that is not enough, the mind needs to learn to stop feeding the ego. But ego is not the word for arrogance as we define it in our daily lives.

In Buddhism' Ego' is defined a little differently, it is not the sense of arrogance but the sense of self. We as human beings have a fragile ego, Why? Because the mind creates the sense of self, and it is deeply aware that it exists because the mind creates it. Imagine a thief pretending to be a respected citizen in front of the cops, and is deeply aware of the crimes he has committed. The fear of being caught, makes him attempt to deceive the cops by pretending to be a normal citizen. He will do anything in his power, to pretend to be 'not a thief'.

Similarly, the ego is the thief, it is deeply aware of all the crimes it commits every day. The crimes like creating a fake sense of self. Attaching itself to greed, lust & pleasures. To make immense efforts to avoid painful experiences. It creates hatred, and creates disgust to suffice itself. The whole cause of suffering is that the ego is unsatisfied, because of the fear of being caught. It reacts to everything that comes around to avoid facing the reality. To understand the attachments completely, we must admit that there are mechanisms of the mind to begin such attachments. What is attachment? Attachment is clinging to something for a permanent support to lean on, but the subject of clinging isn't permanent, therefore the suffering arises.

The attachment begins with data fed to the mind, so it is common sense that there must be a data collection process of the mind. There are data collectors in our bodies. In Buddhism, we refer to them as *The five aggregates* of clinging, which leads to clinging and thus craving. Five skandhas begin the process of attachment, and that is why Buddhism deals with it in its own subtle way. We have this body as a vehicle of life, this living self of ourselves, this is the tool from which we experience this process called life. This tool consists of 5 aggregates, which creates our experience as a living sentient being. These experiences are relevant to be understood before we get to understand the suffering. As per Buddhism, we need to understand all tools, and tricks that our mind uses to bring us to the phase of cravings, and sufferings. Only then we can truly understand the suffering, and go beyond it. After we can study the 5 skandhas, we can begin the practice of awareness of all the aggregates, which will halt creating the sufferings. We have the mention of five skandhas in many Buddhist scriptures. Still, the most important mention was in Prajna Paramita Sutra. It mentioned that Avalokiteshwara went beyond all suffering when she illuminated the five skandhas and found them empty.

Let's discuss the 5 aggregates of grasping, (Five skandhas) in detail.

1. **Rupa-skandha:** This is the aggregate of form. It relates to our physical being, the body and all that leads the outer world to enter us. It is the physical body, which is the first sense of self when we refer to ourselves. The first sense of 'I' begins with the attachment to the body, even when we refer to ourselves in the middle of the conversation we tend to keep our hands on our chest, referring to the body. Though, not referring to only the body, but we will see it in coming sections.

   Through the contemplation of Rupa skandha, we get more aware of the bodily experiences every day. We use the word contemplation and not observation, because observation implies the separation of the observed and the observer, but that is not what will lead us to pure awareness of our body. To reach the pure awareness of our body, we need to observe without the observer. Therefore, it is better to use the word contemplation to be clear with the context. The purpose of such contemplation is to build awareness—and awareness inside of ourselves which remains present all the time, even when we are not meditating.

Most importantly, to lose our attachments with the body because it is not a permanent entity. This is the first way to get to the point of understanding 'what is permanent in us?'. The first step of the process is the outer self, our body. The body's data collectors lie outside, t the eyes, the ears, the nose, the Tongue, the body, and the mind. All this sense collects the data from outside the world. This data gradually covers up our true buddha nature and corrupts our real self.

2. **Vedana-skandha:** This is the aggregate of contact producing sensations. Our rupa skandha gets in contact with their respective forms and thus form sensations. The eyes get a visual, the ear gets a sound, the body gets the touch or actions, and Tongue gets the taste, the mind gets the feelings. All the rupa-skandhas, when in contact with the external world's tangible forms create a sensation. These sensations are the beginning of the flow of the external world to the inner world. These sensations are generated to travel from the outer world to within us, this is how the corruption in the outside world reaches deep in our hearts.

   We are attached to our feelings, and so it is important to contemplate over them only then may we lose the attachment to impermanent feelings, emotions, and sensations. The only way to do it, to meditate, is to relax and view what arises without interference. Which sensations, which emotions, which feelings arise in you, why and when? We are very much attached to the feelings of pleasure. We are attached to avoiding all unpleasant feelings; even the neutral sensation brings boredom, which we try to avoid. After contemplating, you may find out that a lot of what arises inside us is nothing but a reaction to whatever is happening around us. When we observe more deeply, we may realize that our attachment with these sensations are the cause of our sufferings. We need to lose the reaction, and the attachment would disappear.

This separation of pleasant, unpleasant and neutral, makes us want to achieve the pleasant ones while suppressing the unpleasant ones. This 'want' and suppression' leads to so much chaos in the mind. It causes unnecessary suffering within and outside. Then we need more energy to handle the chaos made by this simple distinction of good and bad. The true solution to clear this distinction from within, is awareness. Being aware of the emotions, feelings, and sensations, makes us aware of the reactions and halts the reactions completely. The reactions are not a result of what we truly are. But they are the reactions of what we have become after suffering from everything around us. We experienced the outside world through sensations, & reacted to it. Our reactions created a habit and suffering as well, now the suffering causes more reactions and more suffering. Five skandhas are five layers of impermanence within a human being that could be shed, to reach the true self.

If we are not aware, then avoiding the unpleasant sensation of hard work, sincerity, & learning, will be avoided. Thus the person forever remains stuck in his reactions, & sufferings. The awareness of our sensations helps us come out of this cycle of *reacting to sensations.* After our rupa contributes to the process of data collection, the data turns into sensations. We analyze the feeling of whatever is seen, heard, smelt, or touched, and our minds get into the reactive mode towards all of it.

3. **Samjñā-skandha:** This is the aggregate of recognition. After the sensation reaches us, we tend to give them a name, a definition, and attach these sensations to a particular idea. Such attachment with an idea forms a belief, a thought, a mindset, a habit or a perception.

Such formations allow the mind to imagine a world that is completely different from the real world. The cause of such flawed perception is the covering up of everyone's real being present in the real world. After the external world is collected as data, and turns into sensation, our perceptions try to make sense of those sensations. We get prepared to react to whatever is sensed, and thus we use the thoughts & patterns for attending what is coming. This is where thoughts are formed, ideas are made, and cognition gets into action to attend all the data that need not be attended. The Samjna/Sanna Skandha is the trigger that makes us go down the memory lane on hearing a song, smelling a perfume, or seeing a certain thing. This is the aggregate of association. It allows our senses to make sense of what we have received in the form of data from the Rupa-Skandha and Vedana Skandha. This is the process of pattern recognition, which is so intense that the mind will look for patterns even when there is none. All these causes nothing but suffering to human life.

4. **Samskāra-skandha**: This is the aggregate of mental formations. Here we see the desires, wishes and tendencies to be turned into mental formations. It is described as the state of mind, more like the movement of mind, and causes the movement. Our will, all the actions we do, tend to be followed by more actions, to be called Karma. Karma is the action, cycle of Karma means the action breeding more actions. The voluntary action creates a burden on our Karma. It forms our attitudes towards the decisions of life we make in our tomorrows. It leads us to a certain result of those actions, which were ironically generated somehow by the same actions.
After our ideas, and thoughts are formed, they turn into beliefs, prejudice, & habits. Before we know, our life is spent living in the conditioning of those ideas, that were nothing but a result of the external world getting into our heads. Our true Buddha nature is completely different from what we do in our conditioning. In fact, our ideas and thoughts are actually a cover-up for all that we really are. This is the whole point

of Buddhism, to lose the outer layers formed because of these skandhas, and unveil the leftover, which is the true self.

5. <u>Vijñāna-skandha</u>: Everything we receive, and we do, has an effect on our consciousness. All the preceding Skandhas results in forming this consciousness that leads our day to day life. There exists a pure consciousness completely independent of all the skandhas. Then there is the consciousness that is bred by those skandhas. Our aim must be to renounce one, and to receive another. This Skandha is the fake base created by preceding skandhas, to experience the manufactured information by the data collected by all Skandhas already. If there is not a fake awareness to receive the data, then the play of all the data collection will be over, or it will go on without being received by us. But here we create a fake awareness, attend all such information provided, and thus make sense of it. This is the ego's base, the rigid self that gives us the feeling of 'I' in our everyday life.

When we survive in conditioning, the whole set of whatever we conceived from the world, gets imprinted in our cells and manipulates our consciousness. Our daily consciousness diverts from the ultimate consciousness. It drifts away so far, that we are scared to make an effort to lose all that we are not. We live our lives to suffice the conditioning we manufactured by giving up to the skandhas, without understanding the real process behind it. Though we believe in the idea of meditation, we feel like chasing something so pure is out of our league. It is not; it is just what we must be, truly ourselves, all the time. The universe doesn't need more conditioned beings, it needs people who are true to their nature. Therefore, our responsibility is to reach our true nature by losing all the layers of data that our skandhas have covered up for years of conditioning.

Skandhas are the aggregates of the outer world that play an important role in forming the ego, the 'I'. These aggregates are five destinations in the same path, which leads to the formation of the ego. Simply, these aggregates are how the outer world travels to our inner selves, and corrupts our inner selves completely. Buddhism is the way to stop the unnecessary reactions, so the mind starts contemplating. Slowly, all the layers of makeup, clothes, and fakeness falls off, what remains is the true self.

*"Leave behind confused reactions and become patient as the earth; unmoved by anger, unshaken as a pillar, unperturbed as a clear and quiet pool."*
Buddha

# Chapter- 05
## The Journey of Liberation

*"Know from the rivers in clefts and in crevices: those in small channels flow noisily, the great flow silent. Whatever's not full makes noise. Whatever is full is quiet."*

**Buddha**

Buddhism survived the test of time and became so famous in modern times because it uses common sense behind the suffering of people. The Buddhist scriptures mention that there will always be suffering, cause of suffering, end of suffering & also that there is a way to go beyond this suffering. It's not just human lives, but all forms of life are full of suffering, so we must get out of the life-death cycle and not pray for a better life. We must realize that human life is a better life than all other realms of existence. We must use this life for the best we can do with it. Buddhist scriptures discuss all little topics in detail, with a scientific structure and a sense of understanding. This scientific structure and common sense prove that whoever taught these teachings must have experienced the teachings in their journey. They must have been actually enlightened, to understand such little intricacies in their journey. The person ought to break out of the loop of religious conditioning. The person was no other than Buddha himself. The sutras clearly mention the cause, the effect and the solutions. In this section we will discuss the solution to our suffering. The four noble truths were mentioned in Sutra literature, as the most relevant Buddha teachings, also known as, Dharma-chakra pravartana Sutra.

However, to understand the Buddhist philosophy of life, one must study the four noble truths, and embrace its essence. These steps will help attain an intelligent view on life by realising oneself's buddha nature.

Let us dive deep into the four noble truths, and study their meanings in detail:

1. **Dukkha:** The central theme of the whole Buddhist studies begins with the understanding of the Dukkha. As we translated it, it's the 'Suffering.' It arises from our incapability to satisfy our desires and end in emotional pain for life. Suffering is

painful, and comes primarily with all existing beings. It is one basic feature of lives in all forms, and existence in all existing realms of beings.

Modern society has been built around capitalism. Money is the main motto of life, and luxury is the measure of success. All we want is to jump out in the world, and grab as much as we can. But this habit of getting more and more, does not guarantee any peace. We only focus on getting, sustaining and enhancing the pleasures through the attainment of goals & achievements. But the unavoidable fact is, pleasure and pain are two sides of the same coin, if there is pleasure, there will definitely be pain along the line. Don't be confused. There is a difference between pleasure and joy, pleasure comes from outside, joy comes from within, pleasure comes from materialistic satisfaction, and joy comes from calm. One must seek such solitude that turns into joy every moment. But instead we waste our time seeking pleasure, which is directly proportional to seeking pain. This is the ultimate secret of our life, that has been quite confidently hidden in modern life. There will always be suffering. Physical pain, emotional pain, loss of love, aging body, sickness & diseases, sex & lust, greed & evil, pleasure, attachments & even achievements are all included in this suffering. They are all nothing but suffering, just like Buddha's father had been hiding the concept of suffering from him using luxurious attachments and pleasures. Modern society is doing the same thing to all of us by showing us many things to attach to. There we lose the curiosity to seek or even to begin to seek ourselves. We look so far outside, that we forget to look inside. We are trained to run fast in life. We are taught to live in this illusion that no suffering could chase us if we run fast. But if we all realize the inevitability of sickness, sorrow, & death. And if we truly realize that all of these sufferings are chasing us, no matter how fast we run away from them. We would probably stop running, meet all these sufferings, look at all their faces, all their bases, and then see how, why, and what affects us.

This would allow us to stop and look within, it will allow us to enquire. This inquiry would ultimately lead to one thing, all these things doesn't affect us in any way. It affects the ego, it hurts the ego, and the ego is not 'me'.

Suddenly, the suffering sprouts in our lives because it always does. Then we are shocked, unprepared, unwilling, and upset about it. We are not prepared for it, in fact, we are never prepared for it, But suffering is universal. We perceive suffering on the outer level only, but suffering has various deeper aspects as well. Suffering from change, Suffering from achievement, Suffering from comparison, Suffering from relationships, Suffering from Unknown, Suffering from knowledge, Suffering from illusion, Suffering from running, Suffering from pleasure, Suffering from satisfaction and what not.

The main issue of suffering is attachment. We get attached to pleasure so much that the suffering comes out to break those attachments. Thus, trying to teach us that attachment is suffering. Attachment to happiness, pleasure, lust, greed, & even yourself, is the true basis of suffering. Buddhist scriptures teach us that there are three Suffering levels, Suffering of suffering, Suffering of change, and pervasive suffering. **We understand the first two, but what is Pervasive suffering?**

Pervasive means that is felt throughout our being. Pervasive suffering is the suffering that goes throughout our body and being. It is the attachment to the body and the mind. It could be explained with the help of Five aggregates, which are Rupa (appearance), vedana (sensation), sanghya (labels), samskara (past karma), Vigyana (basic consciousness).

This attachment to these five skandhas (body-mind) is the tool of the endless suffering. In Tibetan Buddhism, there was a great teacher 500 years ago, named Sangkhapa. He explained eight types of suffering: birth, old age, disease, death, contact with anything unpleasant, severance of pleasant contact, unfulfilled desires, and ignorance.

It might come as a shock, and suffering of birth is the biggest suffering of all. The babies get in touch with the consciousness for the first time, enter the world, and instantly experience the suffering of birth. From this point, the cycle of suffering begins. Birth, sickness, death, birth, sickness, death, and it keeps on eternity. Not to forget, there are millions of other sufferings in each cycle, and this birth also could be in different realms of existence. So, nothing is permanent, and nothing is certain. Only one thing is certain: suffering follows life, wherever there is life. Though, all sufferings have certain characteristics, that could help us to understand their nature.

The Four main characteristics of suffering, as per Buddhism are:

- *Anityam:* Anityam means Impermanence. Suffering is impermanent, it does not stay. It comes and goes. Since, nothing in this universe is permanent, everything changes. Life changes, so the suffering in life also must change with life. Everything that seems consistent is changing, at every moment. Sometimes the change is minor. It's not visible to the human eyes. Other times, the change is so dynamic that it experiences while it's happening. Everything is changing. Birth itself is the beginning of dying, creation is the beginning of destruction. The fundamental of everything in the universe is impermanence. All little sufferings will change, and all major sufferings will change. Time heals everything, even sufferings are susceptible to consistent change. It must be enough to bear strength in our difficult times, that whatever we feel today might change tomorrow, and our sufferings would reduce gradually with time.

- *Dukkha:* As we have discussed already Dukkham means, Suffering. This is also the nature of suffering that we end up perceiving it's impermanence as permanence. It makes us forget that the sufferings do not last. This illusion of permanence creates a heavy impact on the suffering, which is even heavier than the suffering itself. This illusion of permanence makes us feel desperate for pleasure. It makes us cling to the pleasant experiences, in the hope of distracting ourselves from the pain of the permanence of suffering. We end up attaching ourselves too much with such experience and people for the sake of having a permanent expected experience. This causes more suffering to be born, and we are again stuck in the same cycle of suffering. As we discussed, once the cycle begins, it becomes impossible to break out of this loop. The more we suffer, the more we seek pleasure, and this seeking of pleasure we often forget that this is a trap. We often forget we must break out fast, and get over this cycle of suffering.

- *Shunyam:* Shunya translates to Zero. In Buddhism, the context means emptiness. Now emptiness might sound depressive to a lot of people. But emptiness does not mean depression. It is not a representation of getting out of life's positivity. Emptiness means zero impact on ourselves, when life gives us pleasure or pain. As we know, both pleasure and pain are equally destructive to our being. None of the two things, brings us true joy. Pain affects us momentarily, and ruins our future decisions. While pleasure provides satisfaction at the moment but makes us addicted to itself and affects our future decisions. Both are momentary, and do not provide a deep impact on our being, though it feels deep. So when we take away this impact of pleasure and pain, what is left behind is the void. The void is what we call shunyam. We can understand it in a different context as well. We all perceive ourselves to be our mind, and our body. When we follow the noble path, and get into meditation, we realize that the mind and body are just the real me layers.

Then the realisation is born which says, Mind and body are not the 'ME'. It brings out certain confusion in us, what is me? The void that is left there, when you take away all that you think is 'ME', that void is the real me. Shunyam, is the state of being, where we drop all outer layers, and remain pure as we are. Shunyam is the state of purity that can be reached through the following eightfold path. Shunyam, is the state of emptiness where a being can reside unaffected from the impurities of life. Shunyam is the state of truth, where the sufferings can take us, if we dare to observe them without being affected by them.

- *Anatma:* We perceive ourselves to be in the body, and the mind. But as we understand, the body and mind are part of the five aggregates' experience, also known as the panch skandhas. In the panch skandhas, there is no self, though they may create a perfect believable illusion. Suffering is created by this illusion of 'I'. Anatma, is made of two words, An, is a prefix that says 'no' or 'not', and' atma' or 'atman', means the soul. Combined it means no soul, or soulless, but not in the literal spooky meaning. We humans consider our soul to be the core of ourselves. It is what we define as the self, so 'anatma' actually implies selflessness. This selflessness can only arise when the being reaches the state of being, after dropping all fale layers of the 'self'. When we reach the stage of shunyam, what we are in the anatma. There is no self to be defined. At least not in the way we defined for all our lives. The true being that you may find in the center, in the shunyam, in the zeroness, is the anatma. Which is not the self, it is not the soul, but it is the empty center. It is not an easy practice to find this center. There will be a fight with depressive thoughts and emotions, while reaching towards the shunyam. This fight will bring out all the emotions of depression that we have ever felt in our lives. These emotions will work as demons of distraction when we move towards our center of the being without covering fake layers created by the environment around us. The center remains unaffected by the outside layers. The five aggregates must be understood clearly, and there is no 'I' in all these aggregates.

**2. Dukkha Samudaya:** The second noble truth is about understanding the cause of suffering. All sufferings have a beginning. Every suffering has a cause, and we must not fight with the suffering but we must focus on preventing the birth of the cause. We all know, prevention is better than cure. If we can observe correctly, it is much easier than fighting the suffering. We must grab the suffering by its neck and follow it to the roots. Only by doing this we may get to the origin of the suffering. Where does the suffering arise? What is the origin of this Dukkha?

The suffering which arises from the root of other causes, all its roots comes alone to a single point, Cravings. Taṇhā or Trishna, is the word that translates to 'Cravings'. These cravings are nothing but our deep desires for attachment. Anything that provokes us to attach ourselves to a goal, achievement, an act, or a person, is a kind of a craving. We must observe this craving, and then go beyond it. This is what the second truth is all about. But this explanation leads to another important question, **Where does this craving come from?** Humans are ignorant beings, we move towards anything that promises a momentary pleasure. This ignorance creates a lot of mess in our lives, this Ignorance breeds desires. This Desire makes us act towards desire, and when we keep acting on its commands, we get stuck so deep in it that it gradually becomes a craving. This craving makes us lose control of our desires and we become a slave to our cravings. Our actions towards fulfilling these cravings are the ones that make the trap stronger. This action leads to a life cycle of suffering.

A famous quote in Buddhism, 'This arises, that arises, this doesn't arise, that doesn't arise'. This implies that we must control the root cause of suffering, and cease the arising of it, rather than focussing on the effects of suffering.

Buddha's theory of human motivation is based on certain key factors shared by all human beings. This motivation is primarily concerned with the nature of human dissatisfaction, discontentment and sorrow. Buddhism teaches us how to understand it, and how to dispel it. In the Sutras, human beings are easily provoked by tanha, which means cravings. Let us dive deeper into Tanha', and understand all its types and features. So, there are three types of cravings:

- *Kama tanha:* 'The Kama' means desire or longing. We may define it as craving, or even better as an attachment to sensory pleasures. The desire for sensory pleasures is known as Kama tanha. Still, Kama often referred to the texts related to sex, as it is the ultimate craving of humans. But we must include cravings for all sensory pleasures. We have different kinds of cravings beginning with cravings of sex, along with the cravings of smell, visuals, voices, or touch. We notice only the sufferings that are caused by negative stimuli. Still, we wish to avoid the suffering that is caused by positive stimuli. In fact, the type of stimuli shouldn't even be a question, if it causes suffering, it is the root of suffering. The only thing we need to do about this suffering, is we need to pluck it out of our lives. Kama tanha is all the desires, & cravings that make us chase pleasure. And avoid pain, even though we have clearly understood that the pleasure is as painful as the pain itself. Our objective to understand Buddhism, begins with understanding the effects of pleasure and pain, the effects of both their sufferings, understanding the causes of these sufferings, and then cutting these causes out of our lives' path. Only by doing this, in the mentioned sequence, we can truly cultivate the lives of eternal joy. This explanation is not about reaching enlightenment. Even Buddhism itself is not only about reaching liberation, but it is also about cultivating joy in our normal lives. Though, that joy can be the first experience of the bliss that we may get from the practice of regular meditation. After we witness it first hand, we could be more motivated to practice meditation, and make it a huge part of our lives. In any case, such understanding only helps us become better human beings.

- _Bhava tanha:_ Bhava tanha, is the attachment to any form of existence. It is basically a craving for survival, living forever, not dying or continued existence. It includes the survival cravings for hunger, thirst and sleep as well. To get a deeper understanding, we may view this tanha, as a desire for power, wealth, property, achievements, goals, success and fame. It is no secret that cravings for sex, money, and power brings suffering in our lives. Buddhism wishes to clarify that the desire for achievement, relationships, entertainment, ideas, opinions, beliefs, and all pleasures is also the cause of suffering in our lives.

This second craving is important to broaden our view about the meaning of suffering. Generally, we consider suffering to be a one-dimensional emotion that can be defined with only one emotion of sorrow, sadness, or depression. But as we discussed, actual suffering is much deeper than that. It is a multidimensional emotion. The cause is different, the effect is different, & even the after-effects are different. This characteristic makes it difficult for normal people like us to judge all true directions of the suffering. We forget to look at it from all angles, and forget to observe it clearly. Thus we get distracted, and we are never able to get out of our cravings. Bhava tanha is different from Kama tanha, in many contexts. Still, the main difference is that Kama tanha is the cravings for sensual pleasure. Sensual pleasures are easy to notice, easy to observe, and could be controlled to some extent. But when we talk about Bhava tanha, the cravings of attachment are hard to notice, hard to observe and hard to correct. Our society is built upon the perception of achievements being the only measure of success. In the race of getting more success, we get more and more attached to our goals, success, and achievements. Once we fulfill or fail in our goals, these goals turn into cravings. These cravings are hard to notice, because the need to achieve more is validated by our society. We want to blend in to fulfill the needs of society. However, once we observe our kama tanha, it becomes a little bit easier to observe our bhava tanha. Only after sincere observations, we can completely let go of this craving, and let go of our need for becoming.

- *Vaibhava tanha:* The three cravings that we are discussing are interlinked, and they move in levels. First, we understand the Kama tanha, then we understand the Bhava tanha. After observing both of these cravings, we get to the third level to get rid of all cravings. It sounds peculiar, but the craving of getting rid of all the craving is the ultimate craving. But it's not as good as it sounds, because this craving can take a wrong path to the wrong destination. Vaibhava tanha is craving for ending the craving through annihilation. The being craves to be non-existent. It asks for self-destruction. It is closely associated with aggression towards our body. When we have a deep wish to harm ourselves physically or emotionally, this violence towards oneself and others is the destructive craving of vaibhava tanha. The one who wrongly believes ourselves to be residing in the body-mind, perceives the end of body-mind, to be the end of all sufferings. This thought could lead the intelligent ones towards a much deeper question, but sometimes it brings the beings to this craving. Which deeper question? The question of the source of this craving. Once this question arises, the beings must start to look for the source and then the game could be played with much fairness and joy.

To better understand these cravings' sources, we must detail something deeper than just cravings. These sources lie beyond the cravings, somewhere close to the origin of all sufferings. Buddhism has given us the twelve links to dependent origination. We will dive deep into these twelve links to dependent origination in later chapters.

**3. Dukkha Nirodha:** Dukkha means suffering, and Nirodha means ending. This third noble truth is all about the ending of the suffering. The cessation of suffering in life The ending of this Dukkha can be attained by renouncing all fake life attachments. Every covering on our beings provides us the feeling of 'I', whatever provides the feeling of ego. Only the ending of this ego means the letting go of the above taṇhā we discussed. The four noble truths gave us a systematic understanding of the problems of the modern man. The first truth explains the suffering. The second truth explains the cause of the suffering. The third truth explains the ending of such suffering. This ending can only be cultivated by grasping the first two truths by heart. Only after completely understanding the first two truths, the third one can be completely accepted. We discussed that 'life is suffering'. This suffering is caused by ignorance. We can see that ending this ignorance will help us end the suffering. Nirvana, is the true ending of all suffering. We must learn to overcome our ignorance of ignoring all the sufferings, and treating them as essentials of life. As per Theravada, nirvana means extinguishing, it implies the extinguishing of the flame of ignorance within us. Once we overcome this ignorance, we end up in a state of being called the Nirvana. Nirvana is the ultimate state of enlightenment. You can reach nirvana, and get out of this suffering for eternity. You may experience the consistent bliss of the universe through this nirvana. One must continue meditation as per the Buddhism teachings, and you end up becoming an Arhat, an enlightened being. As per Mahayana, you may continue meditation and reach full Buddhahood. After attaining Buddhahood, one must continue becoming the teacher for the rest of the world and becoming a Bodhisattva.

As per Mahayana, once the being is enlightened, their ignorance and cravings ends forever. They can never go back to the same ignorance. An enlightened mind might continue for thousands of years in meditation or leave the body when they feel ready for it. Tibetan Buddhism is a sect of Mahayana Buddhism. The goal is to become a Buddha, and then teach them ways to the other beings, to draw them out of their ignorance. The aim is to be a bodhisattva, and draw people out of their sufferings. So the noble truths help us become a buddha and help in awakening the whole world. One important difference between different sects of Buddhism is that, in Mahayana Buddhism, Buddha might be born in the future again in another life to help others. Still, in Theravada Buddhism, a buddha gets liberated from human life and is never born again.

4. **Marga:** The fourth noble truth is the path to the end of the suffering. The essence of Buddhist teaching lies in this eightfold path. The Noble Eightfold Path, is the path leading to renouncing all attachments, cravings, pleasures, and ego. To help us move towards the final cessation of suffering. This path is to implement the above cessation of Dukkha through the ending of all tanha. This is a clear eight steps process of ending the suffering and reaching the liberation. It provides clarity towards the path of enlightenment. Every step of this path is a step towards liberation. Towards the end of suffering, towards an ideal being, and towards a better world for humanity. Before we dive into the eightfold path, we must understand the three basic categories of the eight steps,
let us dive into it:

1. *The Wisdom Path:*

   The first category of the eightfold path is the wisdom path. This category has the first two steps which allow us to align our perception. These are the preparatory steps for walking the noble path of Buddhism. The teachings don't demand a blind belief in the scriptures, in the Buddha or any supernatural being in the sky to follow these two steps. In fact, these steps are made with a common sense of functioning of the mind. These steps allow us to observe and understand ourselves before we get into this path's next steps. These characteristics take us to the basics of our personality. The wisdom path includes the right view and the right intentions. Both of these steps are the steps of observation. It helps us understand what is within and out of our vision. It allows us to be sure that our observations must arise with the right intentions. Right intentions are the seeds that bring fruit at the end of the journey. We can not skip to the fruit directly, we must begin with the seed first. Right intention is truly the most relevant point to begin the journey, and must not be taken for granted. This category has the steps of the path which is about sowing the seed of wisdom within ourselves. These steps will lead us to the rest of the noble path. The Right view allows us to see our true nature without any biases, attachments, and need for pleasure. The second step in this category, the right intentions, allows us to cultivate the sincerity needed to walk the noble path. These two are the building blocks of the whole journey of the eightfold path. Only after embracing these two we may move to the rest of the journey. These are also the ones that build the courage within ourselves, to be true to ourselves and the path coming along.

2. *The Ethical Conduct Path:*

   This section of the noble path includes all the right decisions that influence our daily lives. We saw in the previous two steps that we work on our view and intentions. In these next steps, those intentions will help our decisions move forward to righteousness. This category of the noble path includes, The Right Speech, The Right

Action, and The Right Livelihood. These three factors are the ones that keep a check on our daily life actions, our lifestyle, and our decisions. Some things that we do everyday become the main factors of shaping our lives and our future. If we get into these acts without right intentions, without right notice, and without right observation, then we may do evil acts towards others through our daily decisions. This section allows us to observe, and correct our daily life habits. When we completely embrace the wisdom path, the whole eightfold path gets easier. First we must walk the first two steps, and our daily life behaviour automatically gets a positive impact. Therefore, it is safe to say that the wisdom path leads our ethical conduct. It helps us move towards an ideal life. It forces us to see the world rightly, and live with the right intentions while living our daily lives, with all the necessary action.

3. _The Mental Discipline Path:_

After synchronising our views, our intention and our daily acts, we now need to move to the right practice. The above two paths help us embrace the right mindset and allow us to reflect that mindset in our actions. All these paths are interlinked to each other. The right mindset is reflected in the right actions, and through the right actions, we reach the right practice. By the word practice, we mean practice of meditation. Practice to reach the liberation from suffering. The Mental Discipline path includes the Right Effort, the Right Mindfulness, and the Right Concentration. These three parts help us build a mental discipline necessary to move towards meditation and gradually advance to liberation. This comes as a third section, because it is relevant to clean our mind from all the outside world's clutter before reflecting the clean actions. Then we move to act clean, and then we stop adding more garbage in our minds. Only afterwards we come to the start of the journey of meditation. If you look closely, all three paths reflect the purpose of the journey of meditation. Through this mental discipline, we align our efforts to gain concentration and mindfulness. In this way, we create a lifestyle that is meditative in itself. We start living a life full of awareness, and we live mindfully from all our beings. Our perception of life and the living changes.

Now we have understood this classification, and we have gained insight into the broader perspective of the eightfold path. We have seen three sections that describe the meaning, practice, and purpose of the eightfold path's noble eight steps.

*"Strive to understand what underlies sufferings and diseases – and aim for health and well-being while gaining in the path."*
*-Buddha*

Now we must be ready to take a closer look at each step. These eight steps are the essence of Buddhism, if someone understands these eight steps, they have understood Buddhism's most relevant part. Any Buddhist meditation practice requires clarity in four noble truths and the eightfold path, therefore we will be discussing it in detail. Let's get to it:

Let us get into the central teaching of Buddhism, the noble eightfold path:
1. **Right View:** The first step of the eightfold path, is the seed for the whole journey. This seed will decide the fruit of the whole effort. This is the step to cultivate the right view, or we can say to cultivate the right understanding of life. This is a relevant step to gain an insight into the true nature of reality. The Right view means to gain a positive, compassionate and a kind view for the whole world around us. As we will study in the five aggregates (The five Skandhas) section, some aggregates create filters in our views and alter reality before reaching our vision. This first step is to correct the same errors created by those filters. We cultivate the right view, to be able to see things as they are without the interference and judgement of any aggregates.

When we can see the true nature of the world, situations, people, beings, and the whole universe, that is the right view. When we can see beyond the filters of our mind and make sincere efforts towards being unbiased, non-judgemental, & non hateful. Those efforts will be the effort to move towards the right view. The right view as the name suggests, is to have a correct view. Imagine, there is a lot of dust in your eyes, not only it will be painful, but it will also be impossible to see whatever is in front of us. If we wish to see things clearly, we will need to wash our eyes with cold water. Similarly, five skandhas & other things are consistently building a powerful layer of dust in our vision. We are unable to see the world as it is. We are full of judgements, biases, hate, and other prejudices, towards others. We need to wash our mind's view with some cold water, only then we can cultivate the right view. After we clear this vision, we can move on with our journey, of the eightfold path. We all are aware that the first step of any journey is the most essential, and it has the power to decide the fate of the whole journey. Similarly, our journey of the eightfold path depends solely upon our cultivation of the first step. Even though it seems difficult, it is the steering wheel of the whole way. Every other step depends on the quality of our efforts invested in the first step. Without the right view, we can not cultivate right intentions, speech, etc. Right view is the beginning of an ethical conduct for humanity as per Buddhism teachings. The eightfold path teaches us a lot about living an ethical life, and being a good human being. All the points show us the direction for moving in an ethical direction to be a good company for the universe around us. Everyone should inherit a life lesson from this teaching. Without a right view, it is impossible to cultivate goodness in ourselves. For those not looking to embrace Buddhism, the right view is still a good thing to learn to lead a happier life. There is a famous saying, What we think, we become. It is certainly true that our whole personality begins from what we choose to see. To lead a naturally joyful life we need to see every aspect of life naturally, in its true sense, as it exists. Many monks explain the right view by imagining a seed, you wish for the fruit of liberation, the first act you must do is to sow the seed. Once we sow the seed in the soil, we are all set to move towards the fruit.

In the same way, to move towards the fruit of liberation, we must sow the seed of the right view. All the other steps are like nurturing the seed, watering it, and protecting it, but to sow the seed is the most relevant step. It would be ridiculous to skip the right view and work on other steps, in the same way as it is silly to expect a fruit without sowing the seed. All the other steps follow the right view, so, how should we cultivate the right view?

It is a great question. As we know, the right view is the right understanding. We can begin moving towards the right view by using all that we have learnt up to this point in the book. First, we must understand the three universal truths, and then we must understand the four noble truths. By studying these two things, we automatically move a little positively towards the right view. If we know both these things in our daily lives, we end up being in the right view.

Buddhism is very sensible in its structure. There is a concept of continuation of something permanent inside of us, even after we die. This special fact helps one to get the conviction to embrace the right view. Since, every change brings about a struggle, such a conviction makes it worth embracing this struggle. This becomes an opportunity to get in the rightfulness of the being.

Although, the right view is not about forcing all the right things on yourself, it is more about understanding whatever is breeding the wrong. It is important to remind ourselves, that our right view shouldnt be limited to humans, it should expand to all beings and all things. Once we start to practice the right view, our meditation gets easier. Even the right view itself gets easier to cultivate. The right view avoids adding clutter in the mind, and allows it to stop collecting data through the skandhas or aggregates. We must learn to practice the right view within ourselves, through this practice, the other seven steps of the path become visible. Right view is the most relevant step of this path and the only way to make all the other steps easier. Each step of the path leads to the other step. Therefore we must be sincere towards each step's practice to succeed in the journey at the end. Right view is the cop, when you go through other steps of the path, and you get unsure about which way to go, then the right view could help you keep your actions in check. Right understanding of things, or rather true understanding of things, will always lead you in the right direction. And it would not matter if you understand the concept of other parts or not. Through the right view we come to understanding, we come out of the delusion of life, resulting in reactions, greed, emotions etc. Once we come to an understanding, we begin towards the next step.

2. **Right Intention:** The right view leads us to the second step of the noble path, i.e the right intention. Without the right intention, we can never finish any journey of life. For such a pure journey to begin, we need the courage to put sincere efforts in the right direction. Only the right intention could steer these efforts in the right direction. The right direction demands certain sincerity which does not come along without strong conviction. Now, Conviction is something that needs to be built over time, using a little effort every day. Right intention is the concrete foundation of the conviction, which builds sincerity that results in the right direction for the right intentions. These are the links from the right intentions to the use of intentions in our journey.

After we cultivate conviction through the right intention, our aura is purified. Negative vibes, and evil thoughts start leaving us. Though this is only the tip of the iceberg, it is just the beginning. To purify ourselves completely, we need to go through all the steps of the eightfold path. When the right view is practiced, the right intentions follow. When our mind starts to view the world as it is, we can't think of harming anyone, cheating anyone, or even lie to anyone. All ill acts are born out of wrong view, wrong understanding, wrong assumptions, and ultimately give birth to the wrong intentions. But when we have a right view of life, we wish to live an ideally ethical life, then there comes the clarity of intentions. When the mind is set to the frequency of being right, then right intentions arise by itself. Right intentions doesn't necessarily mean the ideal actions as a human. Still, it simply means that there would not be any deceitful actions. There would not be any incorrectness in our behaviour. Though we all know that the correctness comes from practice. The right intention means there would not be any wrongdoings in our intentions. We would not intend to harm anyone. We would not cheat anyone, and we would never think of any evil acts towards others (and ourselves). This way of thinking will help us to live a life that breeds peace. The first few steps in this list's main focus are building a mindset that breeds action of non-harmfulness towards all forms of life and ourselves.

Buddhism is the religion of immense compassion, and compassion comes out of respect. These few steps help us train our minds to build the mindset that will see everything's true nature. After our eyes see the true nature of everything around us, we gradually build respect for their existence. The simpler way to understand the right intention is to think of the Bhavacakra, representing Ignorance, Greed and Aversion, to cultivate the right intention. One must lose all these three poisons. There must be no ignorance, no greed and no aversion towards any being. Only then one could truly say that they have started living with the right intentions.

Many people have a hard time understanding the basics of the word' right intentions', and they wish to find out before they embrace this step. Right intentions are nothing but reducing all the things that negatively impact us and outside us. It can be anger, lust, greed etc, first we observe it through the right view, and then we reduce it as much as our right view demands. This reduction will help reduce similar negative qualities that will lead us to our journey's next steps. Our objective is to make the reduction reach zero, and only then what is left is the 'right intention'. For some people, it is easy to try and cultivate good intentions. Still, for others, it is only possible through the reduction of bad intentions. Both the ways are effective and acceptable, it depends on what suits our nature.

We must realize that cultivating the right intention is not something that requires additional efforts. Still, it is as simple as the right view, to see what is, as it is. Right view is the step towards right understanding, & the right understanding leads to the right intentions. Once we understand how the negative elements arise, we automatically halt their arising. As humans, we have an inbuilt tendency to avoid whatever harms us. Ironically, we have blurred the vision towards negative elements, and thus we can't remove it from our hearts. We can try to understand the true nature of everything that arises out of us as a reaction. This is the way to test the right view, because only the right view can see truly what is there, and makes it understandable within us. This understanding itself, is enough to step into the right intentions to be born. To understand it completely, Buddhism explains the three types of intentions.

- _Renunciation:_ The intention of renunciation. Renouncing is the ultimate act in the noble path. The desire for achieving a luxurious life in society could disappear. It is not the renunciation of the life we have, but certainly the renunciation of any desire, greed, attachment, pleasure or addiction. Once we gather the courage to abandon the negatives in ourselves, it is a great sign of good intentions within us. It is the right way to breed the right intentions to move ahead in Buddhism's noble path. This is the first pillar for good intentions, it helps us kill the materialistic view of our lives, and bring it a little closer to the realistic view of life.

- _Good-will:_ The intention of goodwill means the intention that is created by complete removal of ill-will. Will is important in creating decisions, choices, desires, and attention towards the desires. Ill-will is something that diverts the intentions towards something that harms either us, or those around us. We must undergo a complete cleaning of ill-will. Only by reduction of the evil-wills, we can cultivate goodwill. Goodwill is the second pillar for the good intentions we cultivate.

Renunciation is leaving all the evil attachments. Goodwill is the reducing all ill will that's left in us. The next one is to cultivate more positive will inside us.

- *Harmlessness:* The intention of harmlessness is again nothing but the absence of harmful intentions. Any intention that creates a harmful impact within us, or around us, needs to be removed from ourselves. Once removed, we can see the cultivation of harmlessness within us. Harmlessness does not talk about only living beings, but it also talks about everything in nature. It brings us close to showing respect towards the creation, and all forms of life. After embracing the right intentions completely and deeply, we can move on to the noble path's further steps. The fact is, we can not practice the right intentions without a right view or the right understanding. Also, we can't practice the right speech without the right intentions. Therefore, we must pay sincere efforts to each step of the path, it will only perfect the current step, & will support our next step.

3. **Right Speech:** Right speech implies the use of speech with compassion. The practice of right speech is probably one of the biggest issues in the modern world. We are in the age of networking, social media and every day connections. Our calls, texts, and everything we shout out on social media platforms all come under the right speech. Right speech seems difficult to induce within our habits, but it is actually quite simple. We are studying the eightfold path, a path of eight steps, and we must focus on each step one-by-one. When we work on the first step of right view, we make changes gradually within the deep sects of our heart. Right view prepares the mind for manufacturing the right intentions. Once the intentions are set to the right frequency, the right speech follows. In fact, we can't force ourselves to embrace right speech. If we are speaking the sweet words but having ill intentions, then it is not right speech. The speech that is born out of right intentions is considered right speech. We must first try to define what comes under right speech. What we mean by right speech.

Right speech is the same as other aspects, it is the complete removal of ill-speech from our system. It doesn't necessarily mean to talk spiritually all the time. Still, it means to abstain from angry, hateful, & reactive speeches. We must abstain from using the words that unnecessarily hurt or offend others. We must not say things that bring our reactions to calm, making others angry, not the speech that spreads negativity. Our speech can either be the way to positively impact the world around us, or a negative impact. Again, it doesn't mean to say only optimistic things in our lives and speak the offensive truth if the situation demands.

All individuals inherit a sense of timing while practicing the right view and right intentions. Then they may share the truth at the right place at the right time, without considering how acceptable it sounds. The only way to keep a check on the speech, is by keeping a check on the intentions. If the intentions are true to the right view, then both the intentions and the speech will be inherently right. Though, it helps to understand the concept of the path to be followed. We may discuss the four different aspects of the right speech, to understand its true essence. These four parts will help us understand how to embrace the right speech within our hearts, so we can live without worrying about what to say next. If we have worked well on our view and intentions, then we could just remember these four parts to keep our speech aligned with the rightfulness. Buddha explains the right speech as something 'Beneficial & True'. It doesn't imply we must share whatever we think, or share whatever we know. No, we must share whatever is required, what is appropriate in this moment, and what is totally beneficial. When we talk about speaking something that is 'True', we have considered it after removing all the mind's filters and clutter. Because truth is not something that we consider to be true, but the truth that buddha mentions, is the truth that remains after the clearance of all the clutter from our minds and hearts. Only that 'truth' must be shared with others, and in a situation that makes the truth 'beneficial' for them. When people are angry, they do not listen, therefore it is not beneficial for the truth to be shared with someone angry. Although, different

Buddhists see the rules differently. They all have the right to keep their speech in check, with their own set of values that aligns with their own right view. The truth can sound different with different words, but it ultimately leads all to one system.

<u>There are four parts of the right speech:</u>
- *No lying:* Lying has become more intuitive within us than how it was a few decades ago. The world has seen millions of changes. Everything is going virtual, and it has many benefits and bad effects. People work hard to showcase their social media achievements, but they also lie a lot about themselves. Specially, lies about being happy. You may notice a trend to act happy on social media, but it isn't a trend yet happy in real life. Lying isn't just in the words, but also in how we present ourselves and our lives to others. It can be direct lying, where we say something that is utterly incorrect, and we know it, but we still say it. Sometimes, we do not even see the wish to lie, but we notice that we suddenly lied while explaining something. We lie out of manufactured necessity or habit. If we decide in this moment, we would not lie, it will be difficult to implement unless we begin from the first step of the noble eightfold path. Lying comes naturally when we are living in a society that creates professions that demand lying. it is not easy to abstain from lying, in fact, it is not easy even to catch ourselves lying in most situations. Only a right view can provide the right eyes to catch the lies. The simple thing to remember is, abstain from lying. In our world, it may seem difficult, but we may begin by removal of small lies. We can begin by stopping the need for lies, in our personal relationships bit-by-bit. Put more truth in your day, where it's more convenient. In this way, our heart gathers more courage to share the truth in our daily life. Sooner or later, our hearts will see that truth feels good, and therefore it must be a bigger part of our lives, which is the best way to begin our journey towards the ultimate truth. We begin by saying the truth that sounds pleasant, and thus inducing the truth in our habits. After some practice, we may learn to say the unpleasant truth, but our intentions must be

correctly aligned with our view. This gradual process, even though the truth might offend a few, but intentionally we will never try to offend people with the truth. We will never misuse the truth's power, we will simply share it for others' benefit.

- _No Frivolous speech:_ Many practitioners get confused with the word frivolous. Frivolous just implies useless speech. Imagine your day and think about what you say which could be replaced from your day without affecting your day. After this, imagine the conversations that made you feel tired after you were finished. Think about the conversations that made you angry, or made you feel negative about yourself. Collect all these conversations from your day which you conduct regularly, and it drains your mental energy. These conversations are everything you say related to a useless topic, like what happened in a movie, serial, sports, judgemental talks, biased speech, etc. All these speeches are considered frivolous speech. it is considered a waste of energy.

Buddhism doesn't see it as a sin to talk about sports or movies, but it tends to limit your mind within these talks if done regularly. The eightfold path is there to make you aware of all the little flaws that make your life a suffering without your intention and notice. Frivolous speech is something that we conduct everyday. The frivolous speech includes any meaningless speech, like gossip, memes, attention-seeking, and time-wasting themes. We consume a lot of virtual content every day, and everything we find is there saved inside of us. We share it with others, to let them know how entertaining things we have found. Although there is absolutely no need to share all such things everyday, we still choose to invest our energy to collect and share such content.Let's spend half of our daily energy on such speech. That means we are wasting the energy used to make our internal system function better. Still, every day we choose to invest it in such frivolous speech. Once we realize where we invest our energy every day, it becomes a matter of choice. In fact, many self-help books mention the importance of talking about the right things. We cultivate the mindset of whatever we say, if we say 'I am depressed', enough times, we are prone to feel worse, and we see 'i am happy', enough times, we are prone to feel better. Our speech affects our system deeply. With the reduction of frivolous speech, we can invest our energy & time, towards something useful. We can find something productive towards our future, professionally or personally. And find out the relevant theme that makes us 'want to discuss', find people who want to discuss the same things, and start a conversation. Once we start a conversation about something productive, it is difficult to go back to frivolous topics.

- *No Abusive speech:* We abstain from using any abusive language, harsh words, or provocative tone. If we practice the first two steps of the noble path correctly, our intentions and the view will align our hearts with goodness. Suppose our intentions are only to benefit others with the truth. In that case, there is no point in being reactive, angry, hateful and loud towards them. If we use abusive speech, it hurts our karma and hurts people through sentiments. Our intention is to share the truth without hurting people.

Moreover, they would not understand any part of what is being said. Buddhism is about seeking the truth and sharing it. To share it we must understand all parts of the right speech because speech affects sharing deeply. We need to be aware of our tone, it shouldn't be a loud or angry tone, there is no authority required. Simultaneously, the truth is shared, people have enough conscience to embrace the truth if not understand it completely. We must believe in people's ability to embrace it.

Most importantly, the use of strong words discourages people from understanding whatever is shared. Our intentions are clear, so we do not need strong words. Strong words are needed to maintain authority. When a Buddhist shares their wisdom with the normal people, they shouldn't use strong words, strong tone, or strong language. They must move towards the softer side of the speech, it helps the listener absorb the knowledge. We must not forget that many people are bad listeners in understanding and saving the information. We might remember everything, but would not let it go deeper in our hearts. Abusive speech, may just provide people a license to ignore everything that's being shared. Abusive speech is the sign of loss of wisdom within the individual. Every Buddhist and every beginner must deeply cultivate this ability to abstain from the abusive speech. This part alone is the building block of right speech, especially in our world of social media. Nowadays, everyone goes on the internet to share what they feel, to share their opinions, and comments on some particular event. All our thoughts are out there, becoming the post, comment, or a story to be shared. Abstaining from abusive speech, makes us more accessible to a larger number of people, helping us nourish our personalities for a better future.

- _No Divisive speech_: Buddhism is a great explanation of a community close to being an ideal community. It shows that Buddha had a vision of a community. Community means people who have similar beliefs, or faith, living together while pushing each other towards a better life. Now, Buddhists see the whole world as their home, and every person as a part of their community. In this sense, we must not practice a speech that divides people. Anything that divides people is meant to cause chaos in the world. A division based on religion, caste, color, language, or country, is meant to make people feel divided. Every religion should be to reconcile people as one, and then uplift them towards enlightenment. Buddhism as a religion, does this through right speech. We must abstain from saying anything that divides people, although it's not easy to say things that joins them. But as a Buddhist, we must speak the truth in a form that is soft and understandable. With the right view & intentions, we will be allowing people to see the futileness of all the divisions. It's enough to make people capable of the uselessness of the divisions, and they can decide what they prefer. However, if one can hold people together with the truth, one must do it, and it would be the right speech still. All political speeches are divisive, apart from the famous speeches that are alive even after decades have passed. Some speeches were so extraordinary that they have this essence of non-division and a feeling of combining them to form a better world. People couldn't forget those speeches. They still remember it, and embrace those speeches. This is the power of joining hands with the world, and losing all divisions. All Buddhists must have the right intentions at heart, non-division is one of the right intentions born automatically after the right view. It will never allow our hearts to engage in any speech that divides people.

4. **Right Action:** The right actions implies every act we do with our body. All the steps of the noble path are interrelated. If we cultivate the right intention, it is impossible to act in a harmful way for ourselves and others. But it is still good practice to keep a check on the right actions. We may define the right actions as the wholesome actions that are not harmful for ourselves and others. As a Buddhist, one must use ethical actions to cultivate compassion within and outside of oneself. To keep a check on our actions, we discussed the five precepts already. Now, three of those precepts are valid here, to keep a check on the right actions. Those three precepts were:

- _No Killings:_ We must refrain from taking the life of any sensitive being, including ourselves, other humans, animals, mammals, and even plants, as much as it is possible. As we discussed earlier, this precept trains our mind to respect life in all its forms, within all beings. When we respect life, there arises a respect for nature, and existence as it is. Killing is an obvious act of evil, we realize it as soon we may think about it. But some thoughts are evil, & killer by nature, but we tend to normalise them in our view. Something as simple as the thought of killing a mosquito as soon there is a humming mosquito around your ear. The thought of killing of a dog who is barking at you, or killing of an ant which is in your path, or killing of a bird who poops on your car, or killing of a person who abuses you. All these thoughts are also considered a killing in our minds. We must abstain our minds from such thoughts. Our thoughts are who we are, so if we are not killers, we must refrain from such thoughts. Suppose we are thinking such things, allowing our minds to move in the direction of such violent thoughts. In that case, the only difference between a killer and the thinker, is time. One day, sooner or later, the thought could become an action, and the thinker would not find a reason, or intention behind the action. Though, they have been cultivating such action for years, through their thoughts. So, it is important to prepare the mind to stop thinking in such a violent direction for anything. This practice helps make the mindless reactive, and allows us to live a life free of violence.

- *No Stealing:* No right intentions, will lead one to steal from others. All right intentions deeply consider others' well-being. Taking away from someone without their permission is disrespectful for someone else is struggling to earn it and disrespectful towards ourselves by lowering ourselves so low as to steal. Abstaining from stealing is a little obvious; when you are trying to move towards the noble path, stealing in no way is a noble act. It is good that most of us already recognise it as a harmful act in society and never do something like this even in a normal situation. But what's less obvious is, we consider taking things as stealing. But we somehow manage to justify stealing ideas, concepts, words, and even thoughts from other people, without providing any credit. This is a trend that is very normal on the internet, among the users of social media. Somebody writes a caption on their picture, their thoughts in the post, writing their own expressions, and someone who likes it posts it as their own expressions. Social media has made such a minor act of stealing, almost invisible to the eyes of our hearts. Though, even little poison is still poison, such little acts of stealing makes our heart immune to the feeling of stealing, and normalises it in our eyes. This act can make us unethical in our behavior without providing any time for ourselves to notice, stop ourselves, or change the little thing inside us.

- *No Misconduct:* We must have discussed earlier that we shouldn't get into adultery or sexual misconduct. But here we must take a wider vision. We must not exploit our passion, enthusiasm or excitement towards anything. In Buddhism, there is no mention of refraining from sex. But here we must not misuse the sexual passion for getting pleasure out of a moment of some awful circumstances. Which only means that our power of decisiveness shouldn't fade in a moment of excitement. Choosing to have consensual sex is not forbidden in Buddhism, in any way. But falling into the trap of sexual desires is mentioned as a sexual misconduct. A moment of passion is different from a moment of excitement. Excitement doesn't imply the joy in a good moment, here it implies the flow of the wrong moment. Any sexual act that is not out of love, molestation, desiring, or anything leads to inappropriateness in our heads. Any sexual act that is not born out of love, out of consent, and out of true passion, could lead to a moment of awkwardness, emotional chaos, and emotional suffering. While following the noble path, the purpose is to reduce suffering. We know it is possible only by reducing the cause of suffering. In our modern time, sexual misconduct is among the number one reasons for all suffering within a relationship.

5. **Right Livelihood:** In our modern world, we have all kinds of professions, that could help one make a lot of money, but not all of them are ethical. Some professions are meant to deceive people. Some professions are meant to harm other beings. Some professions just spoil nature, and some professions are just frivolous. Right livelihood teaches us, not to make a living through unethical and harmful means that demeans other lives, emotional state, nature, or ourselves. We can think of the professions which cause extreme pain and suffering to animals. It includes any profession that includes the killing of humans, or animals. A profession that includes inducing pain & suffering in a living being. A profession that induces emotional suffering to other beings, involves stealing from other people, or deceiving others with manipulation is all included in the wrong livelihoods. We may look at the marketing industry, all the marketing gimmicks that brands pull off, observe them, and see how many of them are true to their buyers. You may be surprised that many brands are whitewashing their brands' image and not talking about their true nature. Though, they feel they need to do such tricks, but the truth is that they have set up a

structure that demands deception. If they could fix their structure, then they might not need to deceive anyone. Similarly, all other livelihoods that cause violence, pain, and suffering towards other beings must not be practiced by the one who is walking this noble path of Buddhism.

Some professions require the person to deal with people in a deceiving way, because honesty can cause a huge loss. The problem is the setup of the institutions that are run on lies. Thus the workers are meant to hold the institutions' structure by taking part in lying and deceiving. It helps them at the moment, to save their jobs, and to earn a living. Still, gradually it kills the trueness inside their hearts, and this deceiving becomes their second nature to live this life. Since this is the fourth step of the path, it is obvious that all the earlier steps lead to this step. No killing, no lying, no stealing are the acts that would help one understand the right action. When one embraces the changes made in the first three steps, this fourth one becomes easier. Some jobs fall under the right livelihood but consume your heart, and time. Such jobs leave you with no energy, no time, and no effort to be applied to your spiritual path. You may continue on it and manage the path, or few people switch their living. It is not just about the path, but also about what brings you peace. It is all dependent on the available options and the need of the heart. One must have a sense of trueness to go through such changes. What you can do, you must do. If you are not ready to make such changes, you know that you are involved in the wrong livelihood. It is completely fine, just be aware of the harm your livelihood causes. If you wish to switch to another harmless livelihood, do it when you are ready. In fact, the job switch is a matter of opportunities you receive. So keep looking for opportunity, and keep exploring life, and it will all lead you to be harmless in all the ways you can be.

6. **Right Effort:** The right view, leads to the right intentions. The right intentions lead to right thinking & right speech. The right speech breeds the right thoughts, & the right

actions. These right actions will now become the right efforts, the effects will be seen not just within ourselves, but outside ourselves as well. The intention will be driving the action, and the effort will come out naturally. If the effort doesn't come naturally, we must be aware of the missing efforts, and put in a little more effort every day.

Right effort is all about, removal of unwholesome qualities to cultivate the wholesome qualities. What are wholesome and unwholesome qualities? Wholesome qualities are the qualities that enhance the quality of the being, life and help attain enlightenment. The first two steps make sure that the arising of the unwholesome mental states is avoided, when the arising of negative stops only then can there be something completely positive. The final two are the steps that talk about boosting wholesome mental states' arising, which again helps make our mental states completely positive. Prevention is better than cure. So we must prevent the mind from breeding unwholesome qualities, which becomes difficult to remove after they have manufactured their foundations in our mind. It is easier and more convenient to stop them from entering our minds.

We can understand the right effort through four parts:

- *Samvara:* Samvara translates to 'Restraint'. This part is about restraining our mind from going towards the unwholesome mental states, and stopping them from arising. Avoiding the rise of unwholesome states and unskillful thoughts, which have not yet arisen. This part is not about restraining the sensory experiences as a whole, but restraint them to stir a conditioned process in ourselves. It works to generate the desire to halt the arising of unwholesome mental states. Every time our senses talk, it triggers some part of our brain, taking us back to the moment in the past, where we experienced similar sensory experiences. This is not ideal because we are trying to live in the present with the right effort. All the steps in the noble path, leads us to step away from living in the past. In this part, we will need to structure our will to stop these weeds from growing in the beautiful garden of our minds. Unless we stop them at this part of the process, it gets more difficult to stop them. If we have the will to stop them before they take birth, we do not need to make extra efforts to stop them afterward. This restraint will provide us more energy to be awake throughout the day. These four parts are interlinked and lead to one another. This first one is simply about, not allowing unskillful thoughts to arise. The thoughts that lead us to feel unwholesome within ourselves have to stop their arising, strategically. We must get to the source of their arising, and discourage their making. Only by putting efforts in this direction, we must move in the opposite direction, which will lead us to feel wholesome within ourselves.

- *Pahana:* Pahana translates to 'Removal.' This next step is to cultivate the wholesome mental states and acts by removing unwholesome ones. It is not possible to discourage the making of evil thoughts within our minds. But we can try to complete the first part of this discussion as much as we can, but we would not be 100% successful. Which is the reason why we need this second point because it will be a gradual process. First, we minimize such triggers and thoughts at the source. Secondly, we try to kill the evil thoughts as soon as they arise, so later we do not have to deal with such thoughts, or their consequences. In this step, we eliminate the unwholesome states that have arisen, just abandon them without any attending. They have arisen, if you do not attend them, they will go. Allow them to go. Even after we try to restrain the unwholesome mental states to arise, there might still be some that arise. So we can use fear, distractions, or other tricks to completely remove ourselves from attending to them. We must recognize the unwholesome desire, and immediately stop it from acting, by doing some little act that is necessary and convenient. In this step, we try to generate the will power to hold the unwholesome triggers, down. We cultivate the behaviour of losing attention towards the distraction in our path. We have to be very cautious not to make it a desire, because one desire can cultivate other desires. So, we just have to get rid of our needs to create negative states, and we can move on to the abandoning of the ones that we couldn't stop at making.

- *Bhavana:* Bhavana translates to 'Develop'. After we halt negative states' making, we can move on to the next step by hitting the source and the newly created triggers. Now, we need to develop the wholesome mental state. After killing the negative impact creating triggers, we must now focus on the positive impact creators. These positive thoughts will slowly erase the impact all previous negative thoughts have left on our minds. Since now we have worked on minimizing the creation of negative thoughts, our mind will have enough free space for positivity. These new positive thoughts, skillful thoughts, and productive thoughts, will take the space emptied by the negatives fading. This step will generate the desire for the arising of the wholesome mental states, & also focus on cultivating the wholesome mental states that have not arisen yet.

- *Anurakkhana:* Anurakkhana translates to 'Protect'. After we have successfully created the desire to cultivate wholesome mental states, we may start cultivating and developing the positive skillful thoughts. We can finally focus on generating the strong will to continue the arising of such states. These wholesome states will be created, developed and protected, to continue building the wholesomeness inside. In this step, we maintain the reached states, and we try to sustain those that have arisen in the previous step.

As we mentioned earlier, Buddhism is very simple yet analytical in all its approaches. Even in the sub-classification of the four parts of right efforts, we can see a simplified process. Which asks us to simply stop the creation of the negative, stop its sustenance, help create positive creation, and help its sustenance. This simply could be called the right effort, and would definitely lead to the final destination of the noble eightfold path.

7. **Right Mindfulness:** Mindful-ness, as the name suggests, is to make the mind-fully aware of the life within us, and outside us. It brings us closer to every moment. Right mindfulness has the power to drag us back from the useless thoughts, useless worries, unnecessary fears, and hurtful past. Once we start paying full attention to the present, we start to clearly see the beauty of life. Once we begin to take our awareness from the past, and direct it towards our present. Modern society provides us with a memory of the past, and turns it into fears for the future. In this way, both our past and the future are corrupted. We do not need to keep the corrupted future and past, in our minds. What we truly need is to create awareness that attends the present. As many philosophers have suggested, we only have this moment to live; there is nothing else to live. So, right mindfulness translates to whole body-and-mind awareness. We must remember, the whole purpose of walking the noble eightfold path is to reduce the suffering that resides in human life. Right mindfulness is

A part of the mental discipline path, where we train the brain to learn to be away from the useless thought process and turn inwards to explore oneself. Here we have this method. We can just make our minds come back to the present moment. It is automatically away from the past, worries, fear, future, insecurities & pain. In this way, we are not requesting the mind to step away from all the negative things. Still, we are giving it another relevant thing to look at, so it would not get an opportunity to convince itself to avoid the work.

Right mindfulness needs some homework before acting up, the process is the same as all other steps. We need to work on our reduction of negatives to breed some positives. We will begin with minimizing our greed, aversion, and delusion. After we minimize all the three poisons within our heart, and within our daily practice, only then we can call ourselves to be living mindfully. All these three poisons are the reason for all major sufferings in the modern world. All our insecurities arise from the delusion that we create in our minds. Our aversion towards another cultivates poisonous thinking about them in our heads. Our greed makes us put all our energy and extra efforts towards getting something that looks relevant as per the social norms. Once we get into these poisonous substances' traps, we start making patterns and solutions to get what these poisons demand. That is where the problem gets worse.

Mindful living avoids creating such poisons within and provides the feeling of contentment that is the goal of every meditator. Meditation is the tool to reach millions of great things, contentment and enlightenment are just the top two discussed. Once the mindfulness is fed, and practiced, it starts working as the observer. It observes the body, the actions, the emotions, and it also observes what we practice in our dhamma, and how capable we are of fulfilling our practice. This step can demand the highest sincerity to maintain the speed and quality of the practice. Mindfulness is a pure activity that will take a lot of energy and some efforts to come into automatic practice. Once you become an expert, the practice goes into an autopilot mode. We can notice if we do not follow it correctly. Though it is possible to lose touch with the practice, for a few intervals in between. In such a situation, we must always focus on getting back in the practice, as soon as we can. We shouldn't focus on why we lost track, or how we lost track. What makes the practice stronger is, to remember the purpose and the teaching. If one has these two things in the pocket, it would be easier to find the tracks faster, every time one is lost. Every new path demands efforts. It can be tricky to follow initially, but with the right amount of sincerity and time invested, it can reach perfection. For right mindfulness, there is a phrase by Buddha in the found foundation sutta, "Just to the extent necessary for overcoming the 5 hindrances". Mindfulness, as required to overcome limitations created by the hindrances, enough to walk on this path.

8. **Right Concentration:** This is the final step of the eightfold path. If one has walked the 7 steps with sincerity, they reach this last stage of the path. This one is the consequence of all the efforts put in the steps discussed earlier. Reaching this stage means that we understood the sufferings, & the causes of sufferings. We diminished negative thoughts, cultivated positive ones, cultivated awareness within ourselves, and improved our concentration along the process. We begin the journey of the complete transformation of the mind, break the chain of its usual processes, and end up at the right-concentration. In Sanskrit, this step is known as "Samma Samadhi". There are various meditation practices to excel: concentration, Vipassana & Shamatha are two to begin with.

We can say, we used the first 7 steps to cleanse the mind, and here we direct its attention towards the relevant thing, enlightenment. So, this is the destination, although this is not the step of enlightenment. We cleared the clutter of the mind, and now we can guide it towards a better goal. Here the mind reaches a state of reflection, where all our actions are purified and well guided. We do not need to worry about our distractions. The mind is aware and mindful of the life running around and within. It is totally aware of the suffering, emotions of suffering, the impact of suffering, ending the suffering, & understanding the suffering. Even though the name is Samma Samadhi, it is different from samadhi itself. Although, this is the final stage that we can control and this is the end of the path, as far as we can come. After this last step, we need to continue all eight steps to check the efforts' quality. Gradually, our practice's quality will excel, resulting in excelling our mindfulness and concentration, which is nothing but a great preparation to receive the ultimate samadhi. For modern humans, who are not interested in reaching the state of enlightenment, this eight-step will bring some degree of contentment. Since a lot of garbage is cleared out of mind, and now the mind works better, it has given up its old ways of generating suffering. The human who practices all eight paths, would feel a new joy in their lives, a joy that arises out of lack of suffering. It would not be enlightening, but it will be satisfactory. Buddhist recommends that one go beyond this level and find the ultimate bliss of liberation. But not everyone has the wish, time and sincerity to walk the path beyond this point. One who reaches the samma samadhi feels nourishing vibes throughout their days. Their mind doesn't crave for the poisons anymore, their search would not create chaos in their lives. After reaching this point, they can finally live a life without any craving to be satisfied.

To conclude the eightfold path, we could say that we have seen all the three sects of the noble eightfold path. First, the wisdom path helps us understand the importance of the right view and the right intentions. We discussed that the right view can fix our mindset in the right direction to embrace any good habit in our lives. We also reviewed that the right intentions can help us get through any difficult path in life. Second, we saw the ethical conduct path, which included more of the daily life activities that impact the people around us and us. It has the right speech, right action, & right livelihood, all of which are related to our daily lives' direct impact. Through the right speech, we leave an impact on others, the way we speak is the second most important information people remember after our appearance. The way we act, decides our fate, our decisions and our whole lives.

Most importantly, our livelihood, we spent more than 80% of our adult life working. So we must choose our livelihood wisely, because if we make a mistake it can affect our mental health extremely awfully.The third sect was the mental discipline path, here we get an opportunity to change important aspects of our mind. We get to direct our mind's efforts towards the right direction, we can do that now, because now it is aware of its faults because of the first step. We get to practice awareness for our decisions, choices, actions, speech, and our whole lives, by right mindfulness, which adds a quality of contentment to our lives. Finally, we get to practice heightened concentration to invest our heart and soul in everything we do.

Society has turned into a capitalist structure. Where money, power, and fame matter the most, and it blinds us so much that we spend a huge part of our lives chasing it. Through these practices, our mind loses the ability to create such illusions around things that don't matter. We realize what we actually need to feel content within ourselves. After we practice and excel in these practices, we will live a mindful life, & the life with some inner peace in every moment of it.

"You must love yourself before you love another. By accepting yourself and fully being what you are, your simple presence can make others happy."

Buddha

# Chapter 06

## The Sense of Self & The 12 Links to dependant origination

*"When this is, that is, when this arises that arises, when this is not, that is not, When this ceases that ceases."*

**Buddha**

Everything in the universe is interconnected. We might understand it through science, or may not understand it yet, but everything exists because of something else. We may fight all the wars, induce violence in the world, and do everything that our minds make us do, but in the end it's not worth whatever we achieve through it. None of it is worth it. Most people in the world are driven to live a life that could grab a lot of money. Deeply we all know, money doesn't bring happiness, then what are we seeking. Just money to buy things, or we think earning money will help us buy happiness. We have a very vague understanding of joy and always connect it to cash, luxury, or pleasure. I have friends who spent all their lives chasing money but in the end they had a lot of regrets.

After earning our fair share of bitter experiences in life, we understand that money can not help us feel real joy in our lives. Money could only help us gain some momentary pleasure, which creates a sense of addiction for pleasure within our subconscious mind. Our goal should not be money in any sense. Money is merely another substance that we need for survival, but it need not be turned into life's pursuit. The goal of life must be a joyful living and a heartful life. We must aim to train our mind to live a life without any useless thoughts or worries, and focus on each moment as it comes. Respect each moment as it comes, and live each moment as it comes. If we do not go this way, then we will end up in a life chasing a feeling, a material, a person, or the sensory pleasures. This chasing has the tendency to keep us busy while giving us a feeling of escape for a while, but it cannot give us any peace. This chasing cannot give us any solitude. This chasing will forever keep us stuck in chasing, within this life, and within the future lives as well. Buddhism has discussed many clear analytical methods to understand the life, functioning of mind, and suffering. These 12 links explain our actions that cause the trap, and make us repeat this life to eternity. We will see how we end up circling in samsara, without ever getting out of it. We just change the realms of existence but never escape the suffering. Only the intensity of the suffering changes as per our deserved existence. Why? Why are we stuck? Where do we begin to fall in this trap?

Here we will answer such questions, we will study 12 links to dependent origination. These links are the beginning point of all suffering, beginning of life, and ending life. We will understand these links from three different classifications. First we will go through each link, and understand their individual importance. Later we will understand the two ways of classifying these links. It will give us an idea of the bigger picture of these links. Let us dive into 12 links to dependent origination.

In Buddhism, it is believed that life is suffering. This suffering is believed to have a cause. As we discussed in the four noble truths. But here we will dissect the suffering to its root cause by moving gradually down to the bottom. Understanding four noble truths helps us to bring about such dissection of suffering. It is the most essential step to discover the true self, discover the Buddha nature, and discover the peace within. As per the pratityasamutpada, Buddhism's central dharma doctrine, we have 12 links to dependent origination. These are the 12 links, a chain of steps that leads us to the sufferings of life. We need to understand the causes of suffering, to move on to the solutions of sufferings.

Twelve links to dependant origination:

The links that binds the living beings to cycles of life, birth, sorrow, old age and death (Incomplete)

1. **Avidya:** Avidya or Avijja translates to 'lack of insight', or 'lack of intelligence'. It means lack of intelligence in the context of intelligence about awareness, about all our actions, and decisions. The missing awareness from our lives is the seed of

ignorance. The one who is truly aware of the real nature of everything around us, sees the world as it truly is and there is no ignorance. Though, Avidya means the lack of this awareness. It basically means, Ignorance. This Avidya is represented by a blind woman, who is walking without a view. She is stumbling on her path, hitting the things in her way. She can not walk without interruption or without getting hurt. She has to bear a lot of pain, and hurdles on her way.

Similarly, An ignorant human is totally unaware of the path, and the steps they need to take to complete the journey. Ignorance implies that lack of insight that is naturally existing in the human mind. This ignorance keeps us away from our true nature, from true compassion and true understanding of humanity. The way our society is set up, this ignorance keeps on increasing exponentially.

The first link is ignorance. An ignorant being is not the one who doesn't know, or who doesn't understand something. In the context of spirituality, Ignorance is the exact opposite of knowledge. Ignorance of true Buddha nature, & the need of moving towards the Buddha-nature. To get rid of this ignorance, one must know the importance of wisdom, & the importance of attaining our true nature. If we do not get rid of this ignorance, we are forever doomed to be stuck in the play of this cyclic existence of life & death. Also, it's not just life and death as a human, but as different beings of various existence realms. So we can say that ignorance is the root cause of being stuck in the cyclic existence .To understand it better, we may look at the two types of ignorance:

A. Ignorance of Karma: Ignorance about the cause and effect of our actions, decisions & Karma. Ignoring the effects of our karma in this life, and the results of Karma in other lives.

B. Ignorance of Reality: Ignorance about the buddha nature within us. The ignorance that drives us away from the ultimate reality and keeps us stuck in the trap of illusions.

We must begin our good riddance of this ignorance, if we wish to be free from the suffering of existence in different realms. But what brings ignorance in our nature? Ignorance is the cause of all trouble, but what is the cause of ignorance?

A good question though, Ignorance hides under the umbrella of the ego. Now, ego here is not the arrogance as we generally refer to. Ego means everything that we perceive as the 'me'. We attach to the ego, and the ego attaches to everything else.

In our next links of origination, we will see how exactly the ego arises in us. What are the main causes behind the creation of this Ego, within us. These steps will turn out to be a process of understanding, and removing ego from ourselves. This connection with ego, makes us do anything & everything to suffice the need of pleasure for this ego. It will be an act of pretending that our connection with the ego is inseparable. So we will indulge in all entertainment acts and pleasure acts for the ego. We will use all our energy and awareness towards dealing with the ego. This ego creates so many attachments that it turns into a game of distracting awareness. This distraction causes the ego to be stronger and stronger. The stronger the ego, the stronger is the ignorance. This distraction, attachments, and all our acts, becomes a great push towards the second link of origination, Formations. Ignorance or Avidya, is the most important aspect of the links of dependent origination. if we could fix our ignorant nature, it helps us create a great base to withstand other origination links' impacts.

The lack of awareness makes us step towards all the sensual pleasures, actions, and decisions that lead us straight into the cycle of karma. Our life goes on, just like we explained in the bhavacakra, it is fueled by the three poisons, and keeps going on for eternity. We live and die, we live different lives in different bodies, with different names and personalities. But we are stuck in the same cycle of time, ego, and death. The action or karma cycle keeps us stuck and would not let us out for even a moment. This cycle would not give us any time to contemplate on our actions. Ignorance avoids awareness, and we end up drowned in this ignorance. The karma or the actions breeding action, forever stuck.

Our aim to study Buddhism is to understand how to cultivate some degree of intelligence to understand this ignorance within us, and then get rid of it totally. We must stop walking on our path like blind humans when we have the mind's perfectly working eyes. Avidya is the first link towards dependent origination, this ignorance keeps us stuck in a life-death cycle.

2. **Samskara:** The word 'Samskara' translates to the Volitional mental formations, which means the mind's willful actions. It implies the choices that come out of ignorance. These choices breed more ignorance, and cultivates more action out of the new ignorance, and this cycle keeps going on. Basically, Ignorance breeding action. These volitional formations are represented by a potter who moves his wheel as he creates things from clay. The potter creates a pot of clay, by rotating the wheel, and moving his hands to shape the pot, just how it wants. Our Avidya, is a mental state of ignorance. Which is a form of preparation of the journey of a long path, that will be forever stuck in ignorance. Such mental formations breed a chain of actions. These actions fill our karmic board, and this karmic board is something that will provide us with a new life of suffering after this one will be over. There we will be handling a new series of other formations, some new links of more consequences, living our whole lives under the shadow of ignorance and breeding more action through ignorance. These whole cycles will breed thoughts that will prove to be harmful in the coming path as well. No matter what we do, until we get rid of the ignorance we cannot even take a single step towards liberation. After we get rid of this ignorance, we move to this second factor, we get rid of the volitional formations. The wilful actions that we justify based on our basis will disappear once the ignorance disappears. Samskara is the second link to the dependent origination. These wilful actions through volitional formations will keep us stuck in the cycle of life and death.

The second link to dependent origination is Sankhara, which translates to Volitional formations. These formations are known as the compound Karma. When the karma gets accumulated by all the ignorant actions from the previous link, it results in the willful actions & decisions amongst our lives. Our ignorant behavior keeps compiling the will's actions to suffice the ego. These actions create a heavyweight of the Karma on our heads. These mental formations are motivated by the same ignorance. The actions arise out of the ignorant mind. It is depicted by the potter, who designs and creates a pot out of clay. He uses the hand gestures to design the shape of the pot. Same way our karma acts as the potter and shapes our lives with our own ignorant acts. To understand this chain, we must view ignorance as the link of the previous life. Let us assume that it represents the ignorance we inherited in the previous life and that life ended. Now all the ignorance bred some Karma, now that life has ended and we have a huge pile of Karma to settle. A Karmic board of actions full of tasks that we did, full of the efforts we made in the wrong direction. Now, we need to compensate for the whole actions, with the effort in the right directions. But that life has ended, and now that karma will decide our fate. It will design our consciousness towards the next life. Basically, our life doesn't end with death, it just changes the body based on our actions and our preferences in this life. This is why Buddhist teaching made an effort to explain, what creates desires, what creates attachment, what creates ignorance, and finally, how to get rid of all those.

The central point being, that we need to stop living our lives moving towards a directionless void, that is death. We are born, we waste our times, and we die. This is not the ideal process of a human life, we could have a higher purpose and stop wasting our lives' precious time. Whatever we do, contribute to building volitional formations within our karma. This karma will affect our existence for longer than we can imagine, therefore we must begin by keeping the record clean and living a life that provides a certain amount of deeper authenticity to our present moment while cleansing our future existences. This will help us, but it will also help bring a higher purpose among the lives of people around us. Our karma could help inspire people towards creating a better karma.

It's not an act of greed, to make efforts for moving towards a better Karma, a better existence, or the true self. This cannot be the act of greed because we are not moving towards something worldly, something fake, something full of illusion, or something useless. We are moving towards something real, something that could bring us closer to God's definition. That is the most blissful experience in the universe.

Our ignorance begins to prepare the will to act on our desires to suffice the ego. The more we suffice, the stronger the ego feels, and then this strong ego receives huge piles of karma from these same actions. The mental formation, or the compounded karma, leads to forming the basis consciousness, which will be the next link.

3. **Vijnana:** Basic consciousness that moves from one life to another. We can imagine it by imagining a monkey jumping from window to window. It implies the jumping of our consciousness from one body to another. The Vijnana represents our consciousness's rebirth in a different life, in different forms, with a different mindset. Vijnana is what creates our sensual experience while our six senses come in contact with the world. Vijnana is the seer in us, that watches and enjoys the whole journey of life. But it must not be mistakes with pure consciousness, that is different from all prejudice, bias and senses. Though this consciousness is the one that we feel to be ourselves, it falls in our observation vision.

We can say the true consciousness gets invested in the senses. It treats the senses & their impact as a real nature of the humans, as the real nature of the mind-body experience, But it is not the true Buddha nature, in fact it is a dependant experience that is changing every moment as per the changing environment of the outside world. The impermanence is the first step of observations, which can help us see ourselves' true nature. We may begin by observing the vijnana experiences and losing attachment with the impact of the sensual effects that we experience daily, every moment, our whole lives. The third link to dependent origination is Vijnana, which translates to Consciousness. This is the basic consciousness in us, that gives us a feeling of being alive. This consciousness is the mirror which reflects the whole universe in itself. This consciousness is the hypothetical eyes behind our personalities. Without these eyes, we wouldn't be able to experience life as we do today. Our mind has these eyes to live with a certain level of awareness of what's going on around us. As we discussed this awareness, is not pure awareness. It is corrupted by the senses, and reactions. The purpose of discussing the 12 links is to see them clearly, and avoid the path totally. As we saw above, ignorance is the seed of this chain of dependent origination links. The Mental formations were the plant that came out of the seed. Now consciousness can be the flower on that little plant. Though this example sounds beautiful, the plant is a weed for us. It's a wild weed with the power to poison the soil, and the whole garden. This little plant has two types of flowers on it, the consciousness is of two types.

- *Causal Consciousness:*
  The consciousness that is dependent on the causes of previous actions. The volitional formations that were formed by ignorance, fills the book of our Karma. Once the karma pages are over, we get ready to move to another life. This consciousness takes the heap of all Karma, all our actions, all our decisions, and all our ignorance. This heap is carried as it jumps from one body to another. The whole record is saved. The actions are not forgotten, and the consciousness still has to compensate for all its previous Karma. Therefore, the causal consciousness is the consciousness that has the imprint of our Karma on it. Since this consciousness arises from the causes of the Karma, it is known as the Causal Consciousness.
- *Resultant Consciousness:*
  Resultant consciousness is the one that is born with us. The consciousness that comes to this life, the moment we are born. Since, this consciousness is the result of our previous lives, we call it the resultant consciousness. This is the consciousness that gives us the sense of life. The viewer behind our brain, and the decision-maker

of our lives behind the masks of the subconscious mind. This is the result that we are trying to create by sustaining good karma in this life, so our resultant karma in the next life turns out to be great. The resultant karma enhances the quality of perception. It creates an intelligent being who might have the potential to change the world. The traces of resultant consciousness begins just around the completion of conception in the mother's body.

Now we must try to understand that ignorance is the factor of this life. The mental formations are the factors of this life, but the vijnana is the factor to help the next life. We clearly implied that the consciousness will be shaped better with the ignorance minimized in this life. But from here on, towards the next link, we will slowly move towards the next life. Vijnana is the beginning of the next birth, as we discussed the moment of conception, now next we will move towards the formation of Name-Forms.

4. **Nama rupa**- our sensory experiences are interlinked to create a perception of the life we are living today. Without these experiences, we would not be trapped in feeling that this is the true nature within ourselves. The Vijnana through the combining of all skandhas experience, develops the mind-body connection, which is what we believe to be the LIFE. It is shown by a man sitting in the boat. Which implies the mental capacity as passengers, and this is the mind. Mind steers the boat of the body like the gondola (the boat driver). These Emotions are what creates the flow towards the destination, across the mighty river of cravings. With mind-body sensory experiences comes a bitter craving for satisfaction. It directly leads to the six sense spheres coming into existence.

Buddhism explains that the formation of Name & body begins at the stage of Embryo formations. In the embryonic stage, after a few weeks of conception the consciousness begins. Still, there is nobody to be aware of that consciousness yet. There are no eyes to that body of consciousness, hypothetically. The depiction of the boat represents that the passengers need to cross from one end to the other end of the river. The boat is just a vehicle to move to another side. Similarly, the name & form are just vehicles for the consciousness to move from this life to another.

The consciousness moves ahead from the stage of conception. The egg turns into a being with consciousness, afterwards the preparation of sense organs begin. These sense organs will be the eyes of the consciousness. The tools of awareness that will create awareness of senses, experiences and the world around are full of consciousness.

In this stage the formation of Name and form begins. The name implies all the non physical aggregates, including emotions, feelings, & basic consciousness. Whereas the form implies the physical aggregates of the consciousness, which is the mind-body formation for itself. At the time of conception, when the consciousness first comes into existence. As soon as it arrives, it starts to show the impact of previous karma piles in its current existence, although it takes time to complete the effects. This corrupt consciousness full of the previous ignorance, actions, mental formations, and all Karma notes, end up here in the new life. Within the first few weeks of conception, the secret task to create names within the understanding of this consciousness occurs. The forms get created as the time goes on. There is a saying, that if we believe a lie for too long, it gets imprinted in minute parts of our body. Well consciousness functions similar to the body, regarding this quote. We believed the ego to be the true center of our body, for millions of our previous lives. Even in this life, everyone seems to act to justify the ego to be the center. In short, we are living selfish lives, for a long time. It has been imprinted in our consciousness as well, which is why the idea to drop the ego seems to be impossible when we first discuss it. But when we try to do it, the dropping of ego, is actually dropping all the garbage brought to our consciousness. We feel clean, because the consciousness feels clean. The thing that is left is pure consciousness. But since the ego started much before our understanding, it's difficult and it seems inefficient to do so.

This egocentric imprint came to us for the ignorance of all karma we ever did. This has been imprinted in this form. In contrast, creation of name & form, even before we were born. Which makes it more and more complicated to comprehend. If we could observe all these problems, we would not need to comprehend it to clarify it from our systems completely. Once we clarify our consciousness completely, we realize how polluted it was before this cleaning.

In simple terms, all the basis of our name and form, begins with the corruption in our consciousness. This corruption begins in our karma's evil deeds, which evil deeds we committed due to our ignorance. This is a simple cycle to understand, and not so difficult to begin the cleaning. Though it must be a gradual process, it is extremely necessary to maintain our consciousness's purity. Ignorance creates a pile of Karma, these Karma turns into Mental formations. The consciousness carries these mental formations and karma, to our next life. Here the consciousness creates the Name and form for the current life. This is how our consciousness starts creating the mind and body. This formation of mind and body, will lead to the next link of dependent origination, developing the six senses.

5. **Shardayatan-** The six senses development comes out of the previous link which is Nama rupa. It is imagined as a house with many windows, the portals- the sight, sound, touch, smell, taste, and the mind, five sense organs take data from present life. In contrast, the mind is a repository of all lives, memories, ideas, deep information etc. These six senses arise, and create the illusion of experience. We experience life differently every day. Without these 6 senses, we would not be stuck in our past, we would not be stuck in analysing, and we would not be stuck in consistent chattering. The first few steps to move towards liberation, is to cleanse the six senses. To lose the attachment of these six senses and put a full stop on their data collection process. We must understand how the senses come into being, and how they manipulate our lives. Only then we can truly go beyond the sensory experiences of life. Because we can clearly see that life today is nothing but a

summary of all the sensory experiences we have. Six senses are an important part of human life, we need them to survive, but we don't need them to create chaos in our minds because the mind gets tired of life. The mind feels stuck in an existential crisis, wondering what life means, and how can it be better? After developing these six sense spheres, comes the next point: contact with the world.

This link is the Six sense development phase, after the formation of nama rupa, the sense organs start to develop. Even after the senses are developed, they can't yet be put to use. This link is depicted by an empty house Because the house is built but needs the residents to use it. Similarly, the senses are developed but need the being to be fully developed to use them. These organs are available for one to experience the world. It develops the ability to experience life, objects, and consciousness through these senses.

In this link, the being is in the stage of forming the six senses, but still not ready for their effective use. It's like a radio. The radio signal is a two way process. The sender sends a signal to the radio, and the radio is the receiver of this signal. So, the sender is ready to send the signal, its functioning well. But the radio wont work until the radio is ready to receive the signal. In our case, the signals are ready, the sender is ready, and even the radio is completely prepared. But the radio is turned off. So, the sense will be used when the right time comes. For the time being, the tools are prepared for the right time. The senses are developed and resting until they are ready to comprehend the senses and receive them.

This phase is essential in the beings existence. These senses will shape the life of the being, they will allow the world to be experienced by the consciousness through them. Without these tools, there would not be any experience in the world. No pleasure, and no pain would be so special without the senses of being. This is the only way we can directly contact the environment around us. It is an important aspect of survival as humans and a relevant aspect of our social lives. This contact takes us to the next link of origination.

6. **Sparsha:** Sparsha translates to "in contact". We as social beings live our lives based on our contact with the world. It is represented by a couple embracing. This is the joining link between the senses and the outer world. This sparsha makes interaction with the world possible. It is the real connection between all our six senses and the objects that we sense. By objects we mean, everything around us, including humans, things, feelings etc. So, this link represents contact of sense with sensed objects. This is the dependence that showcases our dependency on sensual touch or contact with the outer world. The world that is known as Vedana, which brings us to our next link. Here the consciousness develops to a level where the sense organs can be put to effective use. The radio is turned on and it starts playing the music. At this stage we have the organs prepared, the objects prepared, and the consciousness fully prepared, to perceive the world & the events.

It is depicted by a couple embracing each other, while lying on the bed in a lovemaking position. The depiction shows fondling of the couple as an intimate act of contact of two physical bodies.

They can feel each other's body, and the act must be full of pleasure. But here the feeling is unnatural, and the pleasure is superficial. It is merely an act of necessity, just like we eat when we are hungry. It does not validate the contact to be an authentic contact of two beings. At this phase, the force in acting is merely a superficial consciousness. This has been corrupted since the past lives. This superficiality travelled through the first ignorance, to the formations, and actions. It rode on our karma, and entered our new life with consciousness. This superficial consciousness kept going through the six senses as well. Now it has reached the point of contact, through the present superficiality. All the cravings, ignorance and aversion, must be enhanced at every excel point of this link. Creating a worse loop for the coming link, while maintaining a higher possibility of being stuck in the same life cycle for the coming million years or more.

All the faculties we discussed earlier, intersect at this point, but still the contact never feels complete. The six senses are at action, the consciousness is at action, and the awareness acts through both the channels, but not entirely and all contact feels incomplete. The reason is the same corruption in our consciousness. There are so many clouds in the vision of our awareness that we are ignorant even with every moment of contact. We do have the cravings of contact formed through our previous karma and ignorance, which makes us even more desperate in this time. Still, we cannot live this moment completely, and it ought to feel like a missing link.

7. **Vedana:** Vedana translates to 'sensations', when the senses comes in Contact with the world, when the shadayatna, experiences the sparsha of the world, Vedana is born. In a way, sensations are born out of contact of senses with the world outside of ourselves. The image is depicted by an onlooker's eye pierced by an arrow> Now the arrow presents the world's impact on our senses and minds. Though, the arrow represents the painful impact of both the pain and pleasure.This link makes us observe the conditioning of the mind, due to the sensations that arise. These sensations are the first real impact that we feel. All the above links we never see or notice, only the sensation are the first things we can observe and notice easily. Because we can feel them through our senses, but we can't feel the senses, so this is the link where we can begin to contemplate our contemplation. It will be easier as a beginner, but we can move to deeper links of dependent origination as we practice. Through these sensations arise our next link which is, Cravings.
There are generally three types of feelings, pleasant, unpleasant, and neutral feelings. As it is depicted by the arrow in the eyes, it shows us the pain in the most sensitive part of our body. Arrow in the eye is the most painful act we can comprehend. The immediate pain of the arrow and the future pain of living without an eye. This pain introduces the sensitivity of the senses. Therefore, this phase is about a sense of a complete sense of all feelings.

Ignorance takes us to the corrupted formations, these formations get on the consciousness and turns to our name & form. The name & form impacts the formation of the sense organs. The contact provides comfort or discomfort to the being. The contact specifies whether any act provides pleasure or pain. All such experiences can be specified into pleasant or unpleasant by the way how the contact goes. Contact is what turns the world into an experience. This experience, as per the judgement of senses can be turned into feelings on its own. When we feel a certain way, our senses start to note pleasant or unpleasant feelings by doing a certain thing.

Every feeling has a different note attached to it. When the sense organs provide this information to the senses, they start avoiding the unpleasant feelings, and start to look for only pleasant ones. Since the pleasant feelings are just a movement of senses that feel good, it creates a sense of goodness, and the sense starts craving for it.

The links now start to form a chain. These points are all interlinked with each other in a straight sequence.

8. **Tanha:** Tanha translates to the Cravings of a human. This is represented by a man drinking alcohol. This link talks about the addiction to the sensory pleasures, which creates the wanting of more similar experiences. The drinking image represents addiction to the demands of the senses. Our attending of such demands makes us fall for the attachment and forgets the addictions' harmful impact.

   Similarly, we completely avoid the remembrance of harmful effects of the cravings of pleasure, making us create a mess within our minds. This addiction factor keeps increasing exponentially, and it keeps shooting desires to the mind to suffice the cravings of satisfaction. But it is never satisfied with these cravings. It is just like sugar, the way sugar affects our body, sugar is harmful for our bodies, but the more the body gets, the more it wants. Cravings are just like sugar, the body keeps saying that it wants just a little more, but ends up taking all that it can. Sooner or later, we realize that it is actually hurting our bodies and we must have stopped in the beginning. But we never realized it, and we never stopped, so now we have additional diseases to take care of. In this journey of spirituality, the same is our minds' condition where cravings are ruining our success and bringing us to failure. Cravings means the attachment to desires. It is the attachment to any good or bad things of the universe. The deepest attachment is to the feature of cyclic existence at the time of death. Cravings of pleasure from the intoxications of alcohol, sex, drugs, sensual feelings, or relationships. As it is depicted by the person enjoying alcohol, it shows that the person is completely lured into the feeling of being drunk. It shows the intensity of the ignorance of that person, who feels that intoxication could solve life's problems. It does feel like we can step away from life by using some sort of intoxicating substances. It gives us a desperate exit from life for a while. Still, it's ridiculous because the exit doesn't let us out, but it lets us into another problem. It is not even a temporary solution to any problem, as we saw the problems began at much deeper levels. Such substances can only provide a desperate sense of detachment from our lives for a very short time. But in reality, it also turns into a huge cause of attachment to these substances' pleasure or experiences. In a deep karmic sense, we are creating bad karma by exploiting the mind and the body, through such acts, the results of our next lives. This resultant consciousness will lead the name, form, and sense for our next lives, which is a deciding factor of where that life would lead.

9. **Grasping (Upadana):** depicted by a monkey reaching for the fruit. It means clinging, mentally grabbing something, some idea, some image, or attaching yourself to a thought. Man becomes a slave to such attachments. This grabbing has four symptoms: attachment to sensual pleasure, attachment to wrong/evil views opposed to dhamma, attachment to mere external ritual without insight into the spirit of the rites or rituals & attachment to a non-existing self (feels of I & mine), all these four symptoms leads to the act of becoming (Bhava).

When the cravings accumulate, they enhance their power over the will of the being. These cravings start deciding the flow of the decisions, and manipulating the actions of our lives. It could take a powerful form of attachment. This craving power can weaken our peace & strengthen the karmic seeds towards another rebirth in some existence form. It could cause the rebirth in a lower realm, where we might have to life a live of punishment, torture or worse sufferings. Grasping is rightly shown by the monkey grabbing the fruit. Our consciousness is ever ready to grab the fruits of momentary pleasures that create bad marks on our karmic boards. Even at the moment of dying, our consciousness keeps grabbing all that it can, all its habits, perceptions, behaviour, and visions. It leaves the body, but it takes a lot with itself, for the next body. Before it enters the next body, the karma decides which direction to send this consciousness. If it has grabbed a lot, then it would end up in a lower realm of existence. But if somehow the consciousness grabs less then it could come back in higher realms. This link is trying to explain to us that we must keep clearing our consciousness as much as we can, in this life. Cleaning anything in our system is always the best thing to do. It rejuvenates our being, and purifies us from within. Although some of us might not understand the concept of this consciousness jumping from one body to another. But we can simply get to this concept as well, just imagine that there is a possibility that science has not explored all dimensions of our mind-body combination. We are not aware of our functions; therefore, we can not maintain or clean it as required, because we don't understand it fully. Buddhism tries to explain the dimensions that have not been discussed scientifically. Even if you discard these assumptions, you may still follow the cleansing process. No matter which way the belief goes, the cleansing always goes in the same direction. It neutralizes all the toxins inside our perceptions, and clarifies our biases.

10. **Becoming (Bhava):** This link is the desire to exist in the body, and suffice cravings. It is depicted by a woman in late pregnancy, indicating that we transform into a new

being because we tend to covet and mental grasp. Thus at the end of life, we become ready for a new one, to be battered with dukkha. This is the process of creation of 'me' in us, this is the process of beginning our part of existence, and becoming what we must become.

This existence is the result of all our karma, and all the links we discussed earlier. Just before the beginning of the next life, the seeds of Karma from our previous lives, get ripe, and the fruits are ready. It depends on us, whether we planted fruits or weeds. This decides which realm of existence we get. How less our cravings and grasping gets decides a lot in which direction our consciousness goes, these are the watering and nurturing steps for Karma seeds. As we discussed in the second link, the compiled karma reaches its fruition when it gets to this point, and it's ready for the deciding moment. It is shown by a pregnant lady because the consciousness is ready to enter into this world. The karma is ready for this consciousness's existence based on all the links and its resultant at this end.

All the 12 links contribute to this final decision. All links provide us an opportunity to have a clean karmic seed, to get to a justified result in the end. This is the point of existence, as we may say the existence is preparing to find a life source. The whole existence is in the form of consciousness. It is waiting to be yielded and come into a form of life. It is waiting to witness a life as per their karma.

Although even the direction is decided, the being can still change its karma's fate through the right deeds. Karma decides the structure set up of this existence, the outer environment, the basic flow and the amount of suffering for life, as per previous life actions. But it doesn't create a structure of life to be followed. In this new life, anything can happen depending on how the consciousness moves through this life, what the being observes, when he decides to leave this ignorance, and how well he puts efforts towards the world's good deeds.

After the existence finalizes this direction, the consciousness gets ready to take shape into a being. A new being is conceived. A new being is ready to enter this world, and create a mark on existence as they must. A Karma ready to be reset, if the actions of the being allows it to stay clean for the duration of their present life.

## 11. Jaati (Birth):

After our becoming takes place, we enter existence physically through the birth. Birth is the process when the consciousness enters its new body. Buddhists believe that the birth of consciousness happens at conception. After completing the stages of sense development and becoming, the actual birth of the body takes place. This birth is an equivalent of a new beginning of a race. The race is full of hurdles, tiring efforts, countless falls, and sufferings. The race can end abruptly any time, and there is no winning from this race.

It is depicted by a woman giving birth to a newborn, pain by the mother and child is a precursor of the dukkha to come. Dukkha like life, loss, aging and death. It implies that a consciousness has moved from previous life to this life. A new life is also a new opportunity to begin a new karmic cycle. The previous karma has provided the result as this life. Though we must be sure, that this karma still has its traces on this life, and on our consciousness as well. Since, there is only the ending of the body, and the consciousness is the same, the one that was corrupted in the previous life. This concept of eternal life and birth cycle need not sound magical because the universe has a law, that nothing is ever created or destroyed. How can a life be destroyed without giving birth to a new creation? The same way, consciousness must be a form of energy that the scientific community can yet understand. Until then all the base it has is only a belief in the theories of the Buddha. Another religion has been closely relatable with the Buddha teachings, in fact, Buddha's teachings were inspired by it, Hinduism. These are the only two religions, which believe in Incarnation. Rebirth is not a tactic to scare the humans, for behaving righteously in this life. It is just a basic science of energy that must be applied to the concept of life. This life is precious, and it has always been precious. This is a race, but not by won, it's a race to become the best, it's a training. Once we train our consciousness to reach its best potential, that is when it doesn't need to come to a place, where it doesn't belong. It doesn't have to come to a place of suffering, since it is not what it deserves. Though it can handle all sufferings, what's the point of handling these suffering? If not to train to get out of them one day. To bear all the sufferings is a requirement of life, if we wish to move ahead in spirituality. It is merely an act to perform, until we reach Buddhahood. But as we know, the bigger fight is with Avidya, or ignorance.

Because no matter what we do, until and unless we are prepared for our first step, no journey can ever be completed. This birth is the first moment of ageing, and we will have only a limited time to fight our ignorance, get rid of all the 12 links, and move towards our true nature. The time is limited, and the act is urgent, even the first step would be enough to help the future lives and make future births better. But unfortunately, we are kept away from the first step, by the first hurdle itself. Ignorance is the sharpest thing we have to fight before we can begin our journey. If we cannot see where to go, we would hesitate to step, but once we clearly see where we are, where we need to go, and where we want to end up. Then all the steps take us towards our destination. The birth is the moment if previously gathered ignorance of the consciousness starts impacting our present lives. By our current birth, this ignorance has been so well trained to deceive us in blindness of the illusion of the pleasures, that we feel too weak to fight it. We don't have to fight it, we just need to acknowledge, address and observe it. We must trust the process. This observation itself will lead to the disappearance of this ignorance. Our birth would lead to the cultivation of awareness.

12. **Jara-Maaran(Ageing & Death)**: It is depicted by a dying person. It is an unknowing craving without an end & it suggests that death is inevitable. Greed, likes and

aversion, take back one to endless cycles of birth and death. There are two physical decays that a human experiences in this life. The first one is ageing, aging begins at the moment of birth. This is the moment when we start to move towards the end of our time. This decay does not come smoothly, it includes pain, suffering, fear, frustration, anxiety, anger, and weakness. Ageing brings sickness, the body decays and turns weaker everyday. Most people turn to the path of liberation when they start feeling weaker. When they realize that their time is about to be over, they wish to do the most relevant things of life. However, one must start doing the most important things before they are closer to their end. The end is uncertain, and could be closer than we could imagine, so we must begin today. As soon as we see that there is some true ignorance inside us, regarding the true nature of being. We must begin to do something about it, and try to lose this ignorance, right from that moment.

The way we have the society set up, we only see our ignorance after spending a lot of time inside that ignorance. When we become old, we can see it clearly. Though, it could be too late to get rid of it. Which is why, this last link, reminds us of the last link of dependant origination, which is Death.

The depiction showing the corpse, is showing the end of life with the final goodbye. It reminds us that our time here is very limited. The cycle of life and death is a very long chain that needs correction at every link. Death is a very intense subject for most individuals, but it is quite simple in reality. When we watch a movie, we enjoy it, and we know it will end, so we enjoy it more, as much as we can. This is the same logic of life, it ends, sometimes abruptly and sometimes it ends gradually. But we must remember that it ends. Only then can we use today's opportunity to be kinder and honest to people. It's a little peculiar, that we often forget about the end and live a life hoping to continue. Although we discussed the concept of reincarnation, it will be a new life, and we are not sure what personality we will be getting. Honestly, we can only control today, and when we remember death, it gets easier to be kind, and honest. Death is the permanent decay of the body, it is not revived after the consciousness has left the body. With this body, as this being, with this name and this personality, we have a chance to correct our karma, to correct ourselves, and move towards a center of our true nature.

## Conclusion:

These 12 links are the links to our origination in the universe of suffering. We discussed that we have the power to change our origination, and our existence through our cleaning of consciousness. Now these 12 links can be classified in three sections, to get a broader view:

- **Projecting factors:** The factors that project the next links towards the origination. These factors are Avidya, Samskara, Vijnana. These factors are the ones that begin the process of origination. This is the process of planting a seed towards another existence while existing in this life. This does sound magical to some extent, but it has many practical implications when we think about it. This classification is here to simplify the purpose of providing these 12 links to understand why we study these, and why it is relevant to understand them in depth individually.

- **Projected factors:** The origination process begins with the projecting factors, but when we project there is something projected. When we light the torch, there are things that we can see, which were in the dark before. Therefore, when we get into the projecting factor towards origination, something gets projects. The next few links of origination, which we already discussed. Name form, six senses development, Contact and feelings, All these factors are projected by the first few links' projection. We cannot directly influence or manipulate these projections, although we might feel like we can. The true way to influence them, or to stop them from contributing to our origination in this existence of suffering. Since, we have seen through the eyes of Buddhist teachings that life is merely a suffering. To end these sufferings, we must see how the projections work, and what exactly is projected. The development of name, form, and six senses is the beginning of our perceiving of this world. It gives rise to the sensations and contact. Our whole human experience relies on contact and sensations, though when exploited turns into extreme suffering and gets us into the endless existence cycle.

- **Actualizing factors:** The factors projected give rise to the actualizing factors that will realize the real existence. The next links in the chain, craving, grasping & becoming. The previous links of senses, begin the sense of pleasure and pain. This sense brings us to an addiction of pleasure and avoidance of pain. This sense of avoiding pain becomes the biggest craving of our lives. We get into the race of earning more, buying more, achieving more, and attaching to more. Though, we realize very late that all that we get is not going to carry on to the next life. What goes with us in the next consciousness will be our Karma.

These factors help us understand what will be carried, and influence the quality of our next lives. It is not about making us anxious about this life. Still, these factors make us aware of our current mindset and lifestyle. It makes us conscious ethically, we would have intentions to breed the righteous actions within this life's duration. It helps us purify our beings and feel the purity in this life, while helping others feel the same sense of purity.

- **Actualized factors:** The actualizing factors are the ones that are directed by actualizing factors. These factors include the links of Birth, Aging and Death. After we go through all the links, we get to the end of the chain, birth. It is quite funny that birth is considered within the end of the links, the last part of the chain. This chain ends at birth, when the aging of the body starts. The body begins to nourish and move towards the young years, towards the powerful, willful life. Although consciously, we end up decaying the body, and reaching death, without using the time of life for any purpose that is purer than the impure actions of life. We are often motivated by the wrong intentions and the wrong purposes. When we see this chain of origination, this is the time when we completely understand the origin of our actions. Finally, we can view what's wrong with the way everyone lives their lives. This classification helps us see the 12 links in the light of four sections. From here on we can get a deep purpose of beginning towards understanding and avoiding the links altogether.

The 12 links have causes from past lives within the Ignorance and Samskara. The present life effects includes the name, form, consciousness, sensations, contact, becoming,grasping, craving, and six sense.Finally, the future effects are included in the final links of Birth, aging and death.
These links get us to view the past links, the present links, and the future links, repeating themselves for eternity.

*"There is no path to happiness: happiness is the path."*
**Buddha**

# Chapter-07

## Purpose of Meditation & Types of Meditation

*"Don't run after pleasure and neglect the practice of meditation. If you forget the goal of life and get caught in the pleasures of the world, you will come to envy those who put meditation first."*
**Buddha**

As we understood the breeding of suffering through the skandhas, it is essential to clear the mind from all gathered from outside. True peace is when the mind stops reacting. Just like there is a process for introducing chaos to the mind, there is a process to pull it out. Although the skandhas begin collecting data from a very early age, and it is impossible to train ourselves living with an unconditioned mind, our only option remains to clear the clutter as soon as we can. The best way to do it is, Meditation.

Meditation is nothing but the process of allowing every fake element in our personality to fall off by the use of the strongest tool in the universe, Silence. Now, silence doesn't mean the lack of noise. Silence on the outside, is merely one thing that might help the meditation. Still, it cannot be treated as meditation itself. But the silence that is kept and cultivated within ourselves, can be the beginning of meditation. The chaos of the mind begins with the ego, which is formed by sensory experience of the world around us .Though meditation can be difficult if the ego has built strong attachments to activities, images, and people. But once the silence is embraced, it starts to clearly see and starts to STOP REACTING, and Begin contemplating. We have already discussed, Buddhism mentions that contemplation is the necessary step towards meditation, although concentration is the second. By mixing contemplation with concentration we get this balanced dose of silence, which is enough to take the first few steps towards meditation. My friend Rob, works in an IT company as a project consultant, and he lives a very stressful life. He wanted to seek some peace within. I recommend him some simple meditation, a breathing exercise. Once he started doing it regularly, he said that he felt 'a little smooth on life'. The simple meditation helped him handle his wife and kids with much more love, and he felt energized at his work. Though he never thought that meditation could affect his life in so many little ways, when he did it sincerely, he found some affects.

Buddhism has many different ways to meditate, one must try all and see which one suits them. But we have a thief to catch, and they despise the law. The law is meditation, it brings justice to the whole, but they do not want to be caught. Therefore, the beginning of meditation is always difficult. We need to trick our minds to like it, and get through the first few weeks without stopping. The more we teach our mind to like it, the better it feels after meditating. Gradually, it starts losing itself, losing the garbage. When meditation starts working, the mind gets immense clarity on life, actions, & decisions.
Buddha's main teachings include the importance of attachment, and the importance of losing all attachments. The purpose of meditation was to make the mind detached from everything to become free. As we know, our current way of living is not free. It is attached with so many things that we need first few weeks of meditation, to see all the attachments.

Our lives are led by all the content we gather from the Skandhas. Our lives are full of direct and indirect sufferings, which makes us experience life that could be avoided for receiving life in a better way. The way we live our life today, it is like life beats us around all the time. Our lives throw us in the corner, punch us often, and we flow wherever our decisions throw us. It happens because all our decisiveness is born out of corrupt content that we discussed earlier. Though if our mind was silent, free of all corrupt content and totally natural. It would not be disturbed by the corrupt content of the outer world, it would act in its purest forms all the time, and that form would help it flow in life wherever it wants. It sounds like a superpower, but it is just a natural state to be in. In such a state, pleasure feels normal and pain feels normal, everything feels like a nice part of life. Everything feels like a smooth flow of transitions in events, which does not bother the peace we breed within. To breed this silence, we need to begin practicing meditation, like Buddhists do, and it is not as difficult as it sounds. Let us see the most followed meditations of Buddhism. Different types of Buddhist meditations that you can practice are as follows:

- **Metta:** The most famous meditation in Buddhism is compassion meditation, which is also known as Metta. This is the Loving-Kindness meditation. This meditation is what makes Buddhists stand out. The world perceives the Buddhists to be calm and compassionate, because they practice such meditations that bring compassion in our world. It is not possible to love other humans if there is no love in our hearts for ourselves. Metta and Tonglen, are two similar meditation practices with the same purpose. We can either practice one or even practice both, it is our choice. This practice enables us to direct all our love towards our inner-selves and gradually expand it to others. This practice is in sync with the Buddha teachings and also found as the essence of the Yoga Sutras of Patanjali. So the practice is as old as the yoga sutras, or even more ancient as it has its virtues deeply rooted in the Indian Scriptures. One of my colleague left his job last year, and create a travel video blog. He often mentioned that his dream was to travel as much as he can. Though when he started he couldn't earn any money. This decision of work switch, made him bitter and stressed. He hated everyone and people started avoiding him. On my recommendation, he started doing metta meditation. After just 10 days, he found himself calmer, and productive. He was channeling all his energy in his work, and he had more compassion for others now.

- **Chod:** Famously known for being practiced by Chodpa (Mad saints). In chod, the practitioner visualizes cutting all its body parts and feeding it to all beings. Though it sounds scary, the purpose is simply to cut off all attachments, and fears. This technique is actually one of the most respected ones in Tibetan Buddhism. This practice is as old as the Tibetan Buddhism itself, being practiced by the daring saints.

- **Tonglen:** This meditation technique is one of the strongest visualization meditations, which is seen as a representation of the Buddhist monks, it is the Compassion meditation. In this method the practitioner visualizes breathing in the suffering of a loved one, any individual, group or the whole humanity. With every inhale, visualize the inhaling of the suffering of those, and imagine the compassion in their heart melts all the sufferings inhaled. With every exhale, send out a part of their compassion or a solution to the problems inhaled. The purpose is to practice the compassion in our hearts using the visualizations, so that our minds get psychologically trained to practice such compassion in our daily lives. This practice was shared by Kadampa Master around 1000 CE, and later published in many books by other Buddhist practitioners.

- **Trataka Meditation:**

  In this one, we use a single point of concentration to practice (a black dot on the wall, or candlelight). The candlelight helps to enhance concentration and is known as Jyoti meditation. We sit and focus on the candle placed straight ahead a few metres away. We observe light, its movement, its calmness, and try to induce it in our third eye. Purpose is to increase the gaps between the thoughts, and inducing more and more silence gradually. The practice can be found in many yoga books written thousands of years ago. It gained popularity in India's spiritual world around 1980-1990, when the Indian sages/mystics started publishing books about this practice. My cousin Ron, who is also a runner, often feels exhausted with life because of personal issues. He feels distracted and doesn't want to accomplish anything. One of his friends suggested this meditatio, and now he feels more focussed towards the next task of the day. Now he says, 'I am never distracted, never!', his concentration is immensely improved, and he is performing better in his professional and personal relationships.

- **Zazen meditation:** In zazen, there are three steps, Concentration, Koan introspection and Shikantaza. The koan is a sign that isn't intellectually stimulating, its plain and simple circle like design. The purpose is to stop the mind is work, and engage it in concentrated silence. Zazen originated from the term, 'Dhyana' or 'Jhana' in Sanskrit, which means focusing and concentrating. The term 'Dhyana', is often used in the description of yoga, in the ancient texts of Indian scriptures. The purpose is to reach Satori, which is a zen term for Enlightenment. Bodhidharma, took the practice of meditation (Dhyana) from India, to China around 5th CE.

- **Taoist Meditation:** In the Taoist meditation, we visualize our inner-selves connecting to the cosmos, chanting or visualizing our inner self, as the deities, and using qi movements. This technique was developed close to the Tibetan Buddhism itself, around 6th CE. The purpose is to connect with the nature inside our bodies, and realize the life force flowing within us. Famous Taoist meditation, also known as ZuoWang, means 'sit and forget', implying oneself's forgetfulness, forgetting the ego. The mind is full of content, and the images, while we sit and forget all the content, the mind becomes empty. Therefore this is also called the meditation of emptiness. I remember meeting a taoist in a monastery, and when I enquired about taoist meditation he said, 'Its not just sit and forget, and sit, forget and clean, the whole process is cleaning', the immense aura in his eyes, made me note his words.

- **Chunxiang Meditation:** This visualization meditation is an esoteric practice of visualizing the connection of the whole universe within ourselves, the visualization of the cosmos in the whole universe with the universe of ourselves within. This is a strong practice for those who believe in the creation as being the god itself.

- **Zhuanqi meditation:** This meditation is also one of the breathing techniques. The main visualization is to connect the breath with the life force 'chi or qi'. Like mindfulness meditation, focusing on one's breathing without disturbing the breath and focusing on its connection with the life force.

- **Neiguan Vision meditation:** Also known as, Inner Vision meditation to visualize the inner deities, as the life force, thought process, and organs of the body. It works as a healing practice using the life force. This meditation helps one embrace the body's nature and make it work to reach the body's better functions by meditating and putting life force in action.

- **Qigong-chikung:** This technique is believed to be more than 7000 years old, originated in China, and practiced by shamanic and gymnastic practitioners. Though, it was first mentioned around 1122BC, in the famous book I-Ching. The qigong meditation is somewhat similar to Tai-chi meditation regarding the bodily movements, and helping the chi flow throughout the body. Still, qigong has strong visualization techniques to begin with (unlike tai chi). The purpose is to enhance the overall health of the being, by focusing on the breath and picturing a golden light, traveling from the first chakra to the root chakra, while healing all the chakras and the body parts.

Qigong is a larger classification of many exercises. Still, it all basically focuses on breathing, using visualization of color, time, and other things. The purpose is to focus on the breath without interfering in it, and then controlling the life force through the breath. Although this is not a breathing exercise, this can be both sitting and a movement exercise that needs to be practiced within the body's free flow. Allowing the body to flow freely, and manipulate its breath itself. While the meditator is just the witness of the process. The practice is said to have healing effects and spiritual growth as well.

- **Tibetan Analytical Meditation:** In Buddhism, there are two types of meditations, stabilizing practices and analytical practices. In stabilizing practices, mantra chanting mindlessly is done. In analytical meditation, rationally looking at all patterns of thoughts and behaviour is done silently. By doing this, the mind gets aware of all its patterns, and thus drops all the seen patterns to become clear and calm.

- **Forgiveness Meditation:** Much like compassion meditation, forgiveness meditation also works by directing the forgiveness from within to outwards. Mostly directed at ourselves, in the beginning and then directed to a person, we wish to forgive. Self-forgiveness is the first step, and directing it to someone else is the second step. Moreover, directing it to the whole universe can be the ultimate goal as we go forward.

- **Bhakti meditation:** Bhakti means praying. The meditation of prayers is a huge part of Hinduism, mantras and prayers are used morning and evening, to be connected with the lord. Chanting the name of the lord, imagining the lord to be connected with our soul, imagining that connection to disappear as they become one. The concept of non duality stands within every meditation technique that works.

- **Anapanna meditation:** It is a form of concentration meditation, a breathing technique. Still, this time the focus must not be on the breathing itself, but it must be on the air that is inhaled and exhaled. The touch of the air, through skin below nose, then inside the nose, and the more inside you can concentrate the better. The air's touch helps the person begin concentrating on the air, and the breath without manipulating the breath's flow. It was introduced by Gautam Buddha in India firstly, to make the breathing exercise easier for the beginners and thus to introduce the exercise to more and more people.

- **Shamatha Meditation:**In Buddhist tradition, the mind needs to qualify with two abilities: Vipassana and Shamatha. It is practiced by focussing on enhancing concentration, moreover by attaining single-pointed attention. It is also known as Mindfulness Meditation. It is a preliminary step to be followed by Vipassana Meditation, in the Buddhist tradition.

- **Vipassana Meditation:** Vipassana is the main part of the Buddha's teachings and the vision. After following all religious rituals and theological practices, Buddha sat in meditation observing his mind, without interfering. After enlightenment, he realized the way is easier and more effective, he popularized it as Vipassana. It became famous in the west in the last few decades. Vipassana needs utmost awareness and focus, therefore all the other meditative practice sharpens one's focus, so people can later practice vipassana, which is the advanced but easier form of meditation. My uncle who is a theater actor, turned to alcohol in his late thirties, and he got addicted so bad that his wife left him. She filed for a divorce and asked for full custody of both the kids. His fear of losing his kids, made him realize that he has to solve this problem. He went to a class and learnt the Vipassana from a teacher. After two years, today he is living with his wife and kids. He hasn't touched alcohol for two years, and doesn't want to touch it ever again. I asked him, 'how did you get over this addiction' He said to me, 'I was cheating myself, and once we look within, we can't cheat anymore', his words help me to try and move closer to myself, through meditation.

- **Movement meditation:** Yoga is one of the examples of the movement meditation, but all yoga practitioners are not meditators. Tai-chi & Qi-gong also fall in this category. Still, this meditation is not specific to just techniques. Even something simple like walking, dancing, exercise or any movement can be turned into meditative practice. The main purpose is to let the movement guide you instead of guiding the movement. This will help the body be free, and thus, the mind will follow after wandering all that it wants. Tai chi, was first popularized as martial art, but slowly became part of meditation. As the practice itself calms the practitioner, and as the practice goes on, the practitioner becomes the process. Thus bringing silence within the practitioner, which is the ultimate goal of all meditations. Ruby is a yoga teacher, I met her in a yoga class in our city. She often explained the difference between yoga and tai-chi. When she was on a break in the class, and I was about to leave, I stopped to say 'hii'. It was one of those moments when I could ask the expert anything, so I asked. I asked, 'How can you do this all day? Don't you get tired?' and her reply was, 'Of Course I do get tired, but when I move my body feels alive, and this is the only meditation I know, so I am making my own peace', she smiled and got back to her class.

- **Mantra meditation:**Mantra meditation is to meditate using mantras, ancient texts that means something, or only OM. This is a huge part of Hinduism as a culture and prayers. Repetition of a certain mantra with full concentration can allow the mind to drop all garbage and put it in a meditative state.

*"What we are today comes from our thoughts of yesterday, and our present thoughts build our life of tomorrow: Our life is the creation of our mind."*
Buddha

# Chapter: 08

# Buddhist Councils & Buddhist Scholars

*"It is easy to see the faults of others, but difficult to see one's own faults. One shows the faults of others like chaff winnowed in the wind, but one conceals one's own faults as a cunning gambler conceals his dice."*

**Buddha**

*Part 01:* **Buddhist Councils**

The purpose of discussing different types of meditation is to make people believe that they can pick anyone, and begin doing it. The meditation where you sit, and breath, is an advanced practice and thus not recommended for the beginners (although it's a personal perception, which one is more difficult).

In the first week, the goal of practicing meditation is to make meditation a part of your daily ritual. The whole purpose is to find 5 minutes from the day, and do something called meditation. We mentioned many practices here, which are great time-savers, and easy like a play. They are great for preliminary practice. After you can make it a daily ritual and extend the time a little bit every week, you must move on to the next level of practice.

The history of Buddhism is not only about Buddha's life and his teachings in his life. Buddha's enlightenment was meant to change the world's perspective on enlightenment. It was a single middle-path to understand life and its meaning. It was a consolidated form of Hinduism and yet very different from it. Strangely, none of Buddha's teachings were ever written down, even after 100 years of Buddha's death. The disciples of Buddha, started writing and sharing the teachings to their disciples, and gradually the number of disciples grew. There have been many relevant events that get the credit to help spread Buddhism in the world. One such event is the Buddhist council, it was a series of 6 events held in the past that was meant to discuss Buddhism's teachings and relevance. These councils have played an important role in the rise of Buddhism. It is relevant to study these to completely understand the history of Buddhism.

1. **First Buddhist Council:**
   Around 480 BC, Gautam Buddha died in Kushinagar, at the age of 80. The first council was held in 483 BC, at Sattapani cave of Rajgriha. It was presided by the Monk Mahakashyapa under the patronage of King Ajatshatru. The main discussion of the council was to preserve the Sutta Pitaka and Vinaya Pitaka teachings.

2. **Second Buddhist Council:** In 383 BC, the second council was held at Vaishali (around the Nepal borders), Bihar (India).It was presided over by the Monk Sabakami, under the patronage of King Kalasoka. The main discussion held around monastic practices, money handling, & some disputes over Vinaya Pitaka teachings. However, the disputes did not solve clearly, so different sects of Buddhism arose, like Sthavira and Mahasangh.

3. **Third Buddhist Council:** In 250BC, Third council was held under the patronage of King Asoka, in Pataliputra. It was presided over by Mugliputta Tissa. In this council, Abhidhamma Pitaka was established completely.

4. **Fourth Buddhist Council:** In 72 AD, the 4th council was held in Kundalvana, Kashmir. It was held under the patronage of Kushan King Kanishka of the Kushan Empire, presided by Vasumitra. It was in this council that Buddhism was divided in Mahayana and Hinayana.

5. **Fifth Buddhist Council:** It was held in 1871, in Mandalay, under King Mindon, presided by Jagarabhivasa, Narindabhadaja, sunumgalasami
   In this council, after examining, 729 stone slabs were engraved with Buddhist teachings.

6. **Sixth Buddhist Council:** In 1954, 6th council was held in Burma, Kaba aye, Yangon, under the Burmese government. It was presided over by PM U Nu. This council commemorated 2500 years of Buddhism, & was celebrated by 500 Buddhist Scholars.

*Part 02:* Buddhist Scholars

1. **Asvaghosa:** In the 2nd century AD, the biggest poet of India was Asvaghosa. He is known as the first Sanskrit dramatist of the world. He published the Buddhist text in

Classical Sanskrit. He wrote books like Buddhacharita, Mahalankar, Saundarananda Kavya, the book about the brother of Buddha named Nanda. He was a part of the court: Kushan King Kanishka as he was the king's religious advisor.

2. **Nagarjuna:** Founder of Madhyamika school of Mahayana Buddhism. He published Mulamadhyamakakarika (write the most important quotes from this book)-which is the fundamental verse on Middle Way). Nagarjuna has played an important role in spreading Buddhism by being a great teacher of Buddhism. He was the one who gave the concept of Emptiness aka Shunyavad. He was born in NagarjunaKonda (Andhra Pradesh) in a brahmin family.

3. **Ashoka:** The great Ashoka, After becoming king, 8 years later Ashoka the great embraced Buddhism and started popularizing it. After years of exploration, he published the Ashoka Dhamma, which can be said as the Buddhist Dhamma structures and information. Ashoka was the main person to popularize Buddhism in India.

4. **Buddhaghosa:** In 5th AD, he was a great pali scholar. He was known as the voice of Buddha. He wrote a lot of texts for Theravada Buddhism. Later, he went and settled in Anuradhapura in Sri Lanka. He has written the famous Theravada text Vishuddhimagga (find the relevance of this text).

5. **Asangha:** He lived in the 4th century. He practiced meditation in solitary retreat, practicing the Buddha Maitreya. He meditated in hardship for six years, but did not succeed. After failures, he left his retreat and left his hermitage.

*"Your purpose in life is to find your purpose and give your whole heart and soul to it."*

**Buddha**

# Chapter 09
# Theory of The Void

*"Anger will never disappear so long as thoughts of resentment are cherished in the mind. Anger will disappear just as soon as thoughts of resentment are forgotten."*

**Buddha**

Shunyata is the *Theory of Void*; this theory inspired the establishment of Mahayana Buddhism.

Nagarjuna was the founder of the Madhyamika school of Mahayana Buddhism, which is also known as the 'Middle-way' School, avoiding all extremities on the way of realisation. In the 2nd century CE, he was born in a brahmin family in Vidarbha, South India. A gifted being with unusual intelligence and a commendable memory. At the age of seven, he joined the Nalanda Monastic University.

There he was ordained and became a monk. He practiced the sutras and tantras to obtain enlightenment. He was said to be known for his alchemy expertise as well, and knew how to turn iron into gold. He used the skill to feed the Nalanda monks during the extreme famine. He became a great scholar and a teacher at the age of 20 & was appointed as abbot of Nalanda. He once defeated 500 Buddhists in an open debate, which gained a lot of popularity for him. He was an abbot, and was deeply concerned for the purity of monastic disciplines. He even expelled 8000 monks, for not keeping the monastic rules standard as expected. Great concern for his students' slow progress made him obtain the most profound teachings of Buddha.

He was aware that Buddha entrusted the Nagas with his most profound ``The Hundred Thousand Verse Prajnaparamita Sutra" (RESEARCH AND WRITE MORE), for safekeeping. He decided to obtain the texts, and used his siddhis to descend to the realms of Nagas (SNAKES).

He made offerings, and taught Dharma to the King of Nagas (SNAKES). In return, he got the teachings he wanted. But the king kept the last two chapters, because he wished for

Nagarjuna to return to teach him more. It is said, the previous two chapters remain unknown to our worlds. Then he traveled to the north, and became a teacher of King Udayibhadra. Practicing alchemy with the king together, they obtained the elixir of immortality. Since then their lifespans merged and one couldn't die without another. For many years, they both lived in peace. King's son, Kumara, wanted to be the king one day. He knew as long as Nagarjuna is alive, he can't be the king. So he asked Nagarjuna to die. He was so compassionate that he agreed to die at the request of the young prince. He tried to cut his head off, but couldn't. Many other similar attempts failed. He explained that he simply doesn't have any karmic causes to die ordinarily. But he said, in one birth he killed an ant while cutting grass, that karma remains. Therefore, only blade grass can cut his head off. His head was cut off. After being cut, the decapitated head said, 'Now I will go to Sukhavati pure land, but one day I will enter this body again to teach.' The blood from the severed head turned into milk. Kumara hides the head, 2 miles away from the body. It is said that the body and head move closer together every year. When they join, he will emerge from the dead, to share his teachings again.

He gave Mulamadhyamakakarika, which means Fundamental verses on the middle way. He presented the poems and offered the theory of Sunyavada. Shunyavad translates to Emptiness.
It is also known as Madhyamika, meaning the middle way, or nih-svabhava, meaning empty of any behavior, identity, or self.
Shunyata, translates to 'Zero-ness', which implies the meaning 'emptiness'. Shunyata is often related to feeling empty, feeling a void, or meditating in all feelings' silence. Though these meanings are close to the real sense, the exact purpose in different sects is quite different. Shunyata refers to the emptiness of self. As we discussed in earlier chapters, the world around us comes to us in a fake form, through the five skandhas. We perceive the world through a lot of clutter. We can only clean ourselves with the practice of meditation. So, when one can experience a state where there is no 'fake perception of self' and feel

empty of this self, that state is known as Shunyata. This is the state where we have managed to drop all covers of personality. We have moved deeper within ourselves. We have no clutter on our minds, and we can finally see the world clearly as it is.

Meditation can take us to such a zone, where we feel a void within ourselves, also known as the ego's ending. In the beginning, it can be thought of as a little scary experience, because we are not familiar with this loss. Though, in reality, we need to be patient and calm with this experience. Since we have not experienced an embracing of this silence within us, we may perceive it as a little depressing. But it is not depressing at all; it is real. The peace that comes from the meditative state of nothingness, brings us closer to ourselves. This point of nothingness is as close as we can get to ourselves.

Everything is full of existence, and so it can be considered empty. But this emptiness is only implying that there is no self, in anything. Everyone is devoid of the self, and the self that we define is not valid. We have discussed and studied it with the help of skandhas, aggregates, and the universal truths. Everything that we define as the self, is the creation of ourselves. Thus, it is not pure, it is not true, and it is not natural. But if we step into the nothingness, we may see that everything beyond our creation is the true self through our meditation.

Shunyata is the destination of a high-quality meditation journey. The word brings us to the roots and gives us hope of excelling in whichever meditation we practice. We can pick any one meditation, and start it with deep sincerity. Once we start excelling in our practice, we will move towards this nothingness. But the words are not to be taken literally, this movement is not a movement towards a dark and empty self. This is just a movement towards losing all the manufactured layers of ourselves. The whole point of practicing any meditation is to find the inner peace that is always residing in us. This peace is found in that nothingness. After losing all layers of 'self', what's left is the nothingness. We exist in a state of flux, moving within the void. Once we start losing the perception of self, we begin enjoying this nothingness.

We must start meditating today, and be prepared to step into this void. This void will not suck you inside a dark scary zone, but instead it will clear out the vision of our mind. It will help us see through the impurities of life. This void is like a backseat of a driverless car, where we can enjoy the ride without any worries. We will be going on the right path, and towards the right destination. We will not be lying there in a lazy phase, but we will be investing our moments in the things that mean the most to us. We will be spending our life inducing quality in each moment. We will live a quality life, full of joy and smiles. This void is not empty as it sounds; it is just devoid of whatever we don't need in this life. But it is full of what we need, joy, and life.

*"Be vigilant; guard your mind against negative thoughts."*
**Buddha**

# Chapter-10

## Simple Buddhist Guide to Happiness

*"If you are quiet enough, you will hear the flow of the universe. You will feel its rhythm. Go with this flow. Happiness lies ahead. Meditation is key."*

**Buddha**

Buddha was the founder of Buddhism, and he suffered from the extremities of the torturous ways of seeking liberation. There was extreme asceticism, celibacy, blind faith or carelessness. Buddha through his experience realized that none of the intense practice will help him reach the answers that he is looking for. He began practicing the middle way, focussing enough on his survival, health and meditation. Only afterward, he could reach enlightenment, the liberation from sufferings of life. His teachings are beneficial to create a happy life.

Comparison is the most underrated suffering in the modern world. Comparison breeds conflict within, and it is not productive as well. It can take up forms like superiority complex and inferiority complex, in both cases the result is suffering within. This particular suffering of comparison breeds other sufferings in the states of competition, achievements, and greed. Greed is also very underrated suffering. We stop to consider greed as greed, if it disguises the need for money, food, or the need to win. The beautiful words that deeply cover up the desire are the ego's resources to help us fool ourselves. Suppose one can stop feeding the ego's greed and stop the sense of comparison. In that case, it indeed becomes more comfortable to enjoy life as it is. It is not the complete view of meditation, but it can be a great beginning. Changing our lives is a long journey, but it is not a journey of time, it is just a journey of right actions, to breed right results without the greed of results. This is the most important fact, without the desire for results. Meditation is the process of silencing the distractions of life; in such silencing, all the comparison, greed, lust, pleasures, and all negative things are sent to the silence. Thus it helps to live one's life completely.

This is the suffering of life, that we are not living. Somehow we are just waiting to live, & all our efforts towards meditation avoid this attachment with a future life that is somehow better than the present moment. Meditation teaches us awareness of the present moment, and the current breath. This is the ultimate act of letting go of any illusions of the mind, which creates millions of life scenarios that would never come true. All we need to learn is how to live now.

To change our way of living, we must understand the impermanence of all situations in life. The impermanence of people, behavior, incidents, achievements, and pain, must be understood as a fact of life. Only after embracing this impermanence, can we move on to live the present moment freely. Without understanding and embracing impermanence, we are often over-analyzing each aspect of life. Over-analysis causes anxiety, and stress. Sometimes we cannot witness this stress, but it is residing there under the shadow of productivity. We keep ourselves busy with millions of tasks to avoid an encounter with any of these unpleasant realities. But it doesn't change the truth. This impermanence will help us to get out of the analysis, and step into this moment. Once we start to pay attention to our present, our past automatically becomes better. If we enjoy our lives better today, then tomorrow will have a joyful history and thus will have less analysis to be worried about. Buddhism is just a series of techniques to embrace impermanence, live presents, and stop fighting the flow of life.

We all live in constant fear of evil things, bad events, and awful people. We try to live a life that avoids any interaction with any evil things. Our life is full of wishes filled with good events and good people. But we must learn to cultivate good thoughts before we expect a good result from life. Life is only filled with consequences to our actions, and we can create good actions beginning at this moment. All of the life that we did not live yet, starts now. We have learned all fantastic parts of Buddhist teachings, and we have learned their significant implications for human life. We can take the most practical instructions and start practicing them in our lives. We use these teachings, to become a better person. The first step of every journey, must lead us to become a better human being. Awakening, Nirvana, or Liberation, could be a secondary goal for the man stuck in the daily struggle of living. First, induce some peace within then we may even think of reaching liberation. Be a good human; this must be the first application of all the teachings learned here.

I hope this book helped you dive deep into the Buddhist teachings. It may have helped you to reach out to a deeper aspect of yourself, and life. You may feel more confident on the subject of Buddhism, and Meditation. You may have gathered useful information about the three universal truths, four noble truths, eightfold path, and twelve origination links.

The chapters must have helped you explore an analytical approach to decode the mind and life circle. It must have taken you on a journey of decoding the mind, and the meaning of this life. We traveled from understanding the origin of Buddhism, to an intersecting point of all the teachings. This book must have introduced a sensible broad view of existence, knowledge of these teachings, and understanding life. We have understood the aspect of suffering, its causes, and the path to its end. Now it's possible to look deeper into ourselves, by stepping into our preferred meditations. We can switch the pace of our lives and allow it not to pursue worldly rewards. Still, We must turn it into a pursuit of calmness. I hope our lives move towards inner peace every day.

Now, every reader must be wondering,

'how can I implement this knowledge to improve my life?'

Start by contemplation. Through what we have studied about Buddhism and five aggregates' psychology, contemplate these facts' relation with your own life. Since it is all very analytical and straightforward, it's not difficult to find the realist relations in these teachings. After we find a vital connection in these facts, our will must move towards fixing this pattern. When we are ready to move towards a solution, we must contemplate the overview of three universal truths: the first part of our solution. It will create a sense of urgency to fix these problems. Later, we must concentrate on the noble truth, and the eightfold path will allow us to be prepared for our new journey. After doing all this, we will be feeling already at peace, with ourselves. The only thing left to do, is to pick a meditation practice and start by doing it a few times a week. Later, we move to practice once a day, regularly. We may have to practice a few different meditations to find the one that brings us into peace. Once we find it, we can continue doing it every day. After we begin to practice, our minds will wander in the content of our thoughts.

The easiest way to bring it back to meditation is to contemplate the need for reflection, as discussed in the Bhavacakra. You may pick any interesting chapter from this book, which could reach the depth of your heart. Through this depth, use the knowledge gained to keep yourself aligned with your contemplation. Soon, you will get comfortable meditating, without any distraction. This is the time to move beyond contemplations and embrace the void. Shunyata will draw you in, and covers will fall off. This practice allows us to see the true self, and shines a light on *what is real and not.*

Once we see the real, we will never go back to the flaws in our perception. Hence, we will keep practicing and keep moving towards more and more peaceful stages through our practice. We will be inside the void, and we will be full of joy.

*"Radiate boundless love towards the entire world — above, below, and across — unhindered, without ill will, without enmity."*

**Buddha**

# Final words

We have learned a lot, but now we have reached the end. This book was a descriptive journey towards a clear understanding of Buddhist teachings. We discussed Buddhism's birth, which helped us understand Buddha's parents, the Birth of Buddha, his life, and his renunciation. We studied the meaning of Buddha as a title, and a clear difference between the different Buddha types.

In the next chapters, we learned a whole lot of new things about Buddhist life. We explained the concept of the Five precepts, aka the Pancasila. It has the factors that help us take our first step towards embracing Buddhism. It also has the idea of Bhavachakra, which is an easy illustration to explain the need for Buddhism in human life. After understanding the primary factors and Buddhism's needs, we moved towards a little deeper Buddhism aspect: Buddhist psychology. Within Buddhist psychology, we studied the structure of Buddhist teachings, the mind, and the first teachings spread by Buddha himself. From there, we moved to, the three universal truths of Buddhism. These truths are essential to understand the flaws in our current society's perception of a human life. In the next chapter, we explore the building of the same flawed perception. We study the five aggregates which create a fake perception of self. These five aggregates help us move away from this phony perception, and move towards the true self. Once we understand the making of this perception, we can work on halting such flawed creation.

We understood the Birth of Buddha, the Birth of Buddhism, the need for Buddhist teachings, first steps towards Buddhism, Buddhist psychology, and the five aggregates. Next, we studied the most important chapter of this book, the journey of Liberation. This chapter includes the two most relevant Buddhism sections, the four noble truths, and the eightfold path. We talk about the four noble truths in detail; we discuss life's aspect within these truths and the easy way to embrace them in our lives.

We moved to the fourth noble truth, the 'marga', aka the path to liberation. We discuss the eightfold approach within the fourth truth. We studied the eightfold path, in detail to help one embrace each step of the course gradually. As we read here, these steps are discussed within the realms of understanding common man, including their lives. They can take away a massive chunk of information with them, to their daily lives.

After these sections, we turn to a bit deeper aspects of Buddhism, beginning with the sense of self. In this chapter, we discuss the interconnection of all beings in the universe. The connections of one being to all its lives, and what creates the dependent origination. Buddhism has given us 12 links to dependent origination. These links help us understand the connections between the previous life, present life and the next life. We saw how our previous life decisions affect our present life, and how it will affect the next. As Buddhism tries to highlight, all the teachings aim to liberate from this cycle of life. Understanding the 12 links of dependant origination takes us deeper into the teachings. It allows us to peep into Buddhism's more profound purpose for all humanity.

As we reach the final section of the book, we try to put our understanding to practice. Here we discuss the purpose of Meditation and different types of Meditation. Once we get familiar with the most common meditation practices, we can pick one for ourselves. We must pick one and start practicing. With all the information that we gathered in this book, all our meditation practice will have a deeper and stronger foundation in our practice. Every practice needs some information, motivation, and inspiration. The book's first sections gave us enough information and motivation; now the final section must provide some inspiration. So we move to the last part, the Buddhist council and Buddhist scholars. The purpose of discussing the councils, is to allow people to understand a clear history of Buddhism. It has traveled 2500 years to reach our vision, now we are fortunate enough to have studied it in this book, we must embrace the knowledge and put it to practice. The Buddhist scholars are the ones who were responsible for keeping the spark of Buddhism alive in their efforts. In short, they are the reason why we have the Buddhist teachings alive today. If they didn't emphasize these teachings, Buddhism would have been lost a long time ago. By studying their names, we are paying gratitude to them for saving all the knowledge for our generations.

One of the Buddhist scholars was Nagarjuna, who was also the founder of 'Shunyavad' and inspiration for Mahayana Buddhism. In our next chapter, we put some light on his life, and his most interesting theory. We study an overview of his work and teachings.

Finally, we discuss the summary of all the books, and a simple guide to happiness which may help make people's lives better.

I hope that everyone who has read this book will feel closer to Buddhism. I hope that they start their meditation practice and use the information they received from this book. I hope all the readers continue to be curious about meditation, life and inner peace. I hope we all continue our journey to create a joyful life for ourselves, and for everyone around us.

## Thank you for reading my book.
## If you enjoyed it, kindly share the book with your loved
## ones.

We hope that you remember the last quote of this book;

*"In the end, only three things matter: how much you loved, how gently you lived, and how gracefully you let go of things not meant for you."*

**Buddha.**

CPSIA information can be obtained
at www.ICGtesting.com
Printed in the USA
LVHW070008220922
728940LV00010B/302